Christine Hertz
& Kristine Mraz

KIDS 1st
FROM DAY 1

A Teacher's Guide
to Today's Classroom

HEINEMANN
Portsmouth, NH

Heinemann

361 Hanover Street

Portsmouth, NH 03801–3912

www.heinemann.com

Offices and agents throughout the world

© 2018 by Christine Hertz and Kristine Mraz

The authors and publisher wish to thank those who have generously given permission to reprint borrowed material:

Cover of *I Don't Want to be a Frog* by Dev Petty and illustrated by Mike Boldt. Copyright © 2015 by Mike Boldt. Reprinted by permission of Penguin Random House.

Excerpt from *Teaching Reading in Small Groups: Differentiated Instruction for Building Strategic, Independent Readers* by Jennifer Serravallo. Copyright © 2010 by Jennifer Serravallo. Published by Heinemann, Portsmouth, NH. Reprinted by permission of the publisher. All rights reserved.

Cover art from *The Teacher You Want to Be* by Matt Glover and Ellin Oliver Keene was adapted with permission from *Cycles and Patterns of Nature*, created by the fifth-grade class of Opal School of the Portland Children's Museum in 2009. Learn more about Opal School at opalschool.org.

Catalog-in-Publication Data is on file at the Library of Congress.
ISBN: 978-0-325-09250-8

Editor: Zoë Ryder White
Production: Victoria Merecki
Cover and text designs: Monica Ann Crigler
Photography: Jesse Angelo and Michael Grover
Sketches: Kristine Mraz
Typesetter: Monica Ann Crigler
Manufacturing: Steve Bernier

Printed in the United States of America on acid-free paper
22 21 20 19 18 VP   2 3 4 5

CONTENTS

Acknowledgments vi

Introduction ix

1 **Teaching Is Heart Work** 1

    Introduction 3

    The Flourishing Teacher 3

    The Empathetic Teacher 8

    The Playful Teacher 12

    The Flexible Teacher 16

    The Reflective Teacher 19

    Conclusion: Glad We Got That All Figured Out 24

    Interviews with Experts:

        Jessica Lifshitz 25

        Sara Ahmed 27

        Chad Everett 29

2 **The Physical Environment** 31

    Introduction 33

    Big Idea: Setting Up Your Classroom: Start with a Blank Canvas, Not a Finished Masterpiece 34

    Big Idea: Let Your Space Reflect Your Students 44

    Conclusion: Take Time to Reflect on Your Classroom and Your Beliefs 53

    Interview with an Expert:

        Julie Denberg 54

3 **The Emotional Environment** 57

    Introduction 59

    Big Idea: Scheduling for Success 60

    Big Idea: Build a Community, Don't Just Manage One 80

    Big Idea: Social Skills Can Be Taught 86

    Big Idea: Supporting Every Child 93

    Conclusion: Rome Wasn't Built in a Day: Kids Won't Learn Everything

        About Your Community Overnight 101

    Interview with an Expert

        Allyson Black-Foley 103

4 Building Curriculum **105**

Introduction 107

Big Idea: Curriculum Should Be Responsive and Intentional 108

Big Idea: Build a Better Teaching Toolbox: Clear Teaching Structures Drive Complex Learning 118

Big Idea: Responsive Teachers Draw from All They Know 130

Conclusion: Assume Success Is Possible When the Factors Are Right 138

Interviews with Experts:

    Annie Dunn 139

    Yvonne Yiu 141

    Kate Roberts and Maggie Beattie Roberts 143

Conclusion **145**

Appendixes **148**

Tips for Family Interaction 148

Annotated First-Day Letter 149

Annotated Letter About Mindset 151

Room Planning Guide 153

Quick Guide to Teaching Social Skills 154

Quick Guide to Dealing with Challenging Behaviors 155

Checklist Template 158

Conference Notes Form 159

Conferring and Small-Group Planning Grid 160

Works Cited 161

Scan this QR code or visit hein.pub/kidsfirst-login to see videos of Christine and Kristi teaching and to access reproducible versions of the appendixes. (Enter your email address and password or click "Create a New Account" to set up an account. Once you have logged in, enter keycode KIDSFIRST2018 and click "Register.")

Acknowledgments

> We don't have to engage in grand, heroic actions to participate in the
> process of change. Small acts, when multiplied by millions of people,
> can transform the world.
>
> —Howard Zinn, "The Optimism of Uncertainty"

This is the always the hardest bit to write because words do not feel like they can encompass the huge debt of gratitude we feel toward the people who nurtured this book into creation.

First and foremost, we want to thank the many, many, many (*many*) teachers we have worked with since writing *A Mindset for Learning*. It was through your thoughtful questions, provoking comments, and amazing classroom practice that this book was born. To every one of you who asked us a question over Twitter, stopped us to talk after a conference, or shared an anecdote from your classroom, thank you—your very way of being is changing the world for the better.

In particular, there were some teachers who were our north stars. People who create such magnificent and beautiful places for children, we felt humbled to be in their presence. It is our honor to share the work of their classrooms with you in the images throughout this book. Thank you, Kelsey Corter, Julie Denberg, Yvonne Yiu, Amy Lynch, Janet Song, Katie Lee, Kathryn Cazes, Molly Murray, and Megan Maynard Jacob.

Additionally, we were beyond lucky to borrow the brains of several experts in the world. This book is graced with the wisdom of Sarah Ahmed, Allyson Black-Foley, Julie Denberg, Annie Dunn, Chad Everett, Jessica Lifshitz, Kate Roberts, Maggie Beattie Roberts, and Yvonne Yiu. This book is made richer and more powerful by your words; thank you for sharing them.

Then there is our team at Heinemann . . . nowhere else in the publishing world is there such a super team of people bringing high-quality, powerful, progressive work into the hands of teachers. Much like the Avengers, each and every person has a unique skill that makes the whole greater than the sum of its parts. Eric Chalek, marketing guru and punner elite, thank you for the insightful and beautiful work you do to make sure this book finds its way in the world. Brett Whitmarsh, social media provocateur and nicest human alive, thank you for the care and attention you showed this project, and to people in general. Thank you, Amanda Bondi for your superhuman talent of fielding every question with calm and confidence. Victoria Merecki, we are so grateful for all you did to keep us organized, on track, and on time. And a huge, gigantic, and awe-filled thank you to Monica Crigler, the design guru behind this book. We wished for a beautiful book and she surpassed our dreams. That brings us to Zoë—editor, cheerleader, joyful human being, friend, and brilliant resource. Thank you for the thoughtful questions, insightful comments, and moments of joy as we worked through this book. Without you we'd still be brainstorming. And probably crying.

We have to thank the pioneers who first settled this educational landscape for us: Don Graves, Katie Wood Ray, Alfie Kohn, Kathy Collins, Steph Harvey, Smokey Daniels, Marie Clay, Matt Glover, and, of course, Lucy Calkins. We owe a special debt of gratitude to Lucy and the entire Teachers College Reading and Writing Project for showing us that "small acts can change the world," and of course, for introducing the two of us.

Christine says

This book would not be in your hands if it were not for Kristi's heart and vision for a better world of tomorrow. I have been lucky enough to think and laugh and cry and write side by side with Kristi as she not only imagines that better world, but also charts out a course for getting us all there. I have also been fortunate to work with brilliant and dedicated teachers, teachers whose work with children is both humbling and inspiring: Maura Kelly Wieler, Colleen Riddle, Megan Maynard Jacob, and Annie Dunn, thank you. A few teachers shaped this book eons ago without even realizing it. Sue Todd, James Newell, Topher Waring, and Viv Buckley: being your student made me a better teacher and a better person. I can't thank my parents, family, and friends enough for all they do, in their corners of the world, to make this a more just, joyful, and kind place, and for all they have done to help me see this book into being. Finally, Nate, I am so grateful for your constant enthusiasm and support through wins, losses, and rains.

Kristi says

I have to thank my coauthor in crime, Christine, from the bottom of my heart. Christine is an incredible teacher, talented writer, and genuinely good human. She is also the MVP of this book, having taken on the bulk of the work when my baby came. Everything good in here probably came from Christine. I want to thank my fearless administration team, Adele Schroeter, Nekia Wise, and Alison Porcelli. They've kept an unwavering vision of what is best for children at the forefront of what they do. A huge thanks to teachers and friends who have made me a better human and a better teacher: Katie Lee, Valerie Geschwind, Kathryn Cazes, Amy Lynch, Kristin Ziemke, Kate Roberts, Maggie Beattie Roberts, and Chris Lehman. I hope you see your footprints all over this book. Thank you to my best friend and partner, Geoff—whenever I think I can't, he shows me I can. He is my better and more brilliant half. I love you always. And finally, thank you to baby Harry who let me write this book during his naps. I will move mountains to make this world better for you.

Introduction

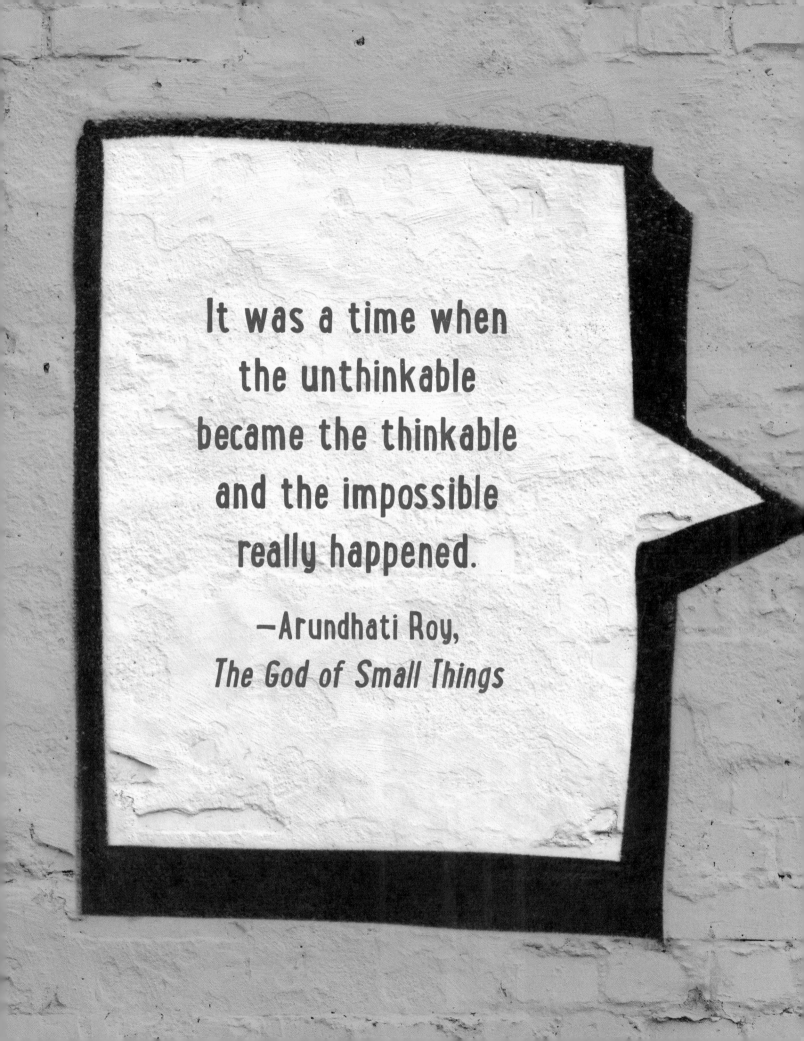

A Tale of Two Classrooms

When Kristi was getting ready to enter the teaching profession, she couldn't wait for the first day to arrive. For her, it was a chance to leave a mark, to impact the lives of children in positive ways, a grassroots, ground floor opportunity to make the world better tomorrow than it is today. She envisioned writing letters to the local government, litter and recycling lessons in the nearby park, and an empowered group of children who would stop at nothing to make positive change. Cut to her first year in the classroom: passion and good intentions only go so far when confronted with the day-to-day intricacies of teaching. Chaos reigned in her classroom.

Overwhelmed, overworked, and feeling incapable of translating big dreams into classroom practice, Kristi decided to try a behavior system commonly called a "clip chart." This chart, made colorful and pleasing to the eye, had all the children's names clothespinned to the top. If a child "misbehaved," his name was moved down (and down and down). Perhaps with behavior in order, her class could take on the projects that would save the world.

At first, it seemed to work! The chaos dulled to a simmer and there was hope she might be able to take on the projects she had envisioned. Then one day, a few weeks after Operation Clip Chart, a seven-year-old boy named Thomas walked calmly to the colorful display to move his clip down and instead tore the entire chart to shreds.

The class was stunned silent. And then there was cheering.

Not from the kids who always stayed at the top of the clip chart, but from the kids who struggled with behavior day in and day out.

As she drove home that night, Kristi felt desolate. In that one move, Thomas had laid bare the real workings of the clip chart. Kristi knew this practice was common—in fact, some of us might use it today. On that drive home, she recognized the nagging feeling (that you might recognize as well) she'd had all along that the crestfallen look on a child's face as she moved her clip down in plain view of her classmates couldn't be what building a classroom community was all about. It had seemed to work, but work for whom? Whose life did it make better? Yes, it was calmer, but why? Not because she had taught great lessons of respect and community skills, but because, all glossing over aside, she publicly embarrassed kids who acted out of step. What if they didn't even know what boundaries they'd overstepped? Could there be another way? Right then she decided: it wasn't projects that would change the world, it was teaching how to be an engaged and responsible member of a community. None of her preservice classes had prepared her to *teach* such a thing, just to demand it. Hence, a decades-long inquiry project was born into the question, how do we create a cohesive and nurturing classroom community, filled with kind, empathic, engaged citizens?

Meanwhile, years later and states apart, Christine thought she was on top of her reading teaching game. She had created an extraordinarily neat and tidy grid depicting which students she would meet with, when. She had lessons planned down to the minute and a list of standards that she could check off as she went. She had a binder of running records for each student and data on top of data on top of data. Her many guided reading groups were providing her students with scaffolded support every step of the way. It was a well-oiled machine. But the problem was, *Christine* was the center of that machine.

One day, Christine was in a professional meeting in the room next door to her classroom. Her students were supposed to be independently reading and she popped back into her room quickly to grab a file. As she looked around the room to admire her industrious readers, it dawned on her: no one was reading. Not one kid. Some students were staring out the window, others were shopping for books, a couple were doodling in their reader's notebooks and one, she learned later, had been in the bathroom for about twelve minutes.

Without Christine at the center of the reading workshop, her students weren't actually interested in reading. Instead of building for independence, teaching for purpose, and creating opportunities for authentic learning, Christine had taught them how to be compliant cogs in a reading machine. There was no joy. No purpose. No intrinsic motivation.

That day marked a powerful shift in Christine's thinking and teaching. She started to reexamine her role and the role of her students. For years she's been thinking and studying how to foster independence, authenticity, and joy in every element of her students' learning.

Finding a Path from the Worst of Times to the Best of Times

Here is the thing: clip charts work, and so does doing nine million highly scaffolded reading groups—for a time. And these systems primarily work *for the teacher*. As we taught, we realized that so much (too much) of the profession is focused on the ways teachers can make students successful, but not how we give children the tools to build their own success day after day after day. Things started to feel *not right* as mandate after mandate came into our classrooms.

Does it matter if our children meet benchmarks or line up quietly if it comes at the expense of engaged, active, curious learning? Passivity makes for easy management—and terrible citizenship. How do we make the classroom more like the world? How do we teach skills like independence, critical thinking, and responsibility? How do we help our students learn in a way that honors their passion and curiosity, yet ensures that they *also* meet the benchmarks they need for success? What would happen in a classroom where children do not have an assigned spot for everything they do? These are the questions we took on in our classrooms, and in the classrooms of our friends and colleagues. We read books and blogs, we read studies and research about the brain and learning, we played in our rooms, we sat with our failures, and we rose to teach again.

Our collective of teachers, armed with studies and professional texts and days and years in the classroom, began to believe that it is the decisions we make even before the first days of school—from how we set up our rooms to how we build community to how we prioritize curiosity and joy—that will determine whether we, and our children, will thrive, not just as students and teachers, but as wholly engaged and alive human beings.

So Where Are We Now?

Kristi has a classroom that (mostly) hums with collaboration and camaraderie. The children in her room have strategies for solving problems, sharing materials, asking for help, and negotiating solutions. Her children regularly talk about empathy and work to make the community and the world kinder. She doesn't yell, nor move clips. Her children have free reign of materials and seats and ideas, yet the chaos is controlled and driven by curiosity and learning. Gone are the rewards, the stickers, the threats, and in their place is a world built on trust and hope and care. It takes work and commitment, patience and time, but from the first moment of the first day, Kristi is teaching the skills of being a member of a community.

As for Christine, students in her classroom are agents of their own learning. From day one, her students make decisions, set goals, build their skills, and fill their toolboxes with strategies that they can use when they need to. Every day she tries to give her students more choice over little things like what book to read and big things like what to study during a class inquiry. Christine is no longer at the center of her classroom's activity; instead she is on the periphery—dipping in and out, coaching students, and making little adjustments along the way. In her classroom, learning is social: joy, play, and collaboration are at the center of every part of her day. Nothing is perfect, but everyone feels empowered to learn and grow.

Come Along with Us

This book is a place to start creating the classroom of your dreams. A classroom that is research based, child centered, and in step with the world today. A classroom that exemplifies the collaboration, flexibility, agency, and problem-solving that people need to be successful in the coming decades. A classroom where critical thinking, thoughtful reflection, and curious inquiry sit side by side with reading, writing, and math, But here's a caveat: we're not going to promise that you'll ever achieve classroom nirvana—we know there's no such thing as perfection. And we are the first to admit that this is hard, messy work. There will be missteps and mishaps, but just like your students, you will learn from your mistakes and grow. Know that there is a community out there ready to celebrate and commiserate and think and question with you every step of the way. This book is just a first step, a launching pad to what is possible. To help you along the way, we've included lots of our favorite books, people to follow on Twitter, interviews with experts, and videos of the two of us teaching.

This book is divided into four main parts

1 Teaching Is Heart Work grounds us in the art and the heart of teaching. The first part of the book will help us tap into our most flourishing, empathetic, playful, flexible, and reflective selves so that we can be the teachers our children deserve. We'll look at the research and the reasons behind cultivating our best selves first. This section is the work that happens before we meet children on the first day and keeps our teaching souls fulfilled. It tints the pages and sections that follow it, and the atmosphere beyond.

2 The Physical Environment and **3 The Emotional Environment** are guides to building classrooms of empathetic, joyful learners. In these sections, we will explore how both the physical classroom environment (from the nuts and bolts of how to set up your room to different options for flexible seating) and the emotional classroom environment (from teaching social skills to handling really tricky moments) set the foundation for your classroom culture and some of your students' most important learning. We'll pull from new research and diverse fields to get beyond the idea of classroom management to the idea of building a community of citizens. This section will be handy as you invent and reinvent your classroom space or delve deeper into building a powerful classroom community.

4 Building Curriculum will help you understand how to study the work and habits of your students and let those observations drive your instruction. You'll find practical tips such as how to make a checklist and quickly assess student work to the justification behind many different teaching structures. We'll look across educational theorists to cull together the must-knows for a teacher building a classroom of cutting-edge practice. This section is best used once you are up and running with students to assess and reassess your teaching moves and potential next steps.

The appendixes, the final section of the book, is a toolkit filled with templates, additional resources, sample letters, and quick guides to turn to.

Though the book does not need to be read in any particular order, each section builds on the ideas previously explored. For example, messages about classroom community and social skills begin with classroom design. Impactful, intimate teaching requires a productive and respectful community. However, where you start might depend on what you need:

Are you looking to infuse or reclaim a spirit of joy and possibility into your teaching? Do you wish your students were happier and more playful? ***Start in Section 1.***

Looking to create a beautiful classroom space that fosters collaboration, independence, and curiosity? Are you curious about the intersection between environment and behavior? ***Start in Section 2.***

Do you want to create a classroom community free of rewards and threats? Do you see a need for your children to learn social skills but aren't sure how to go about it? ***Start in Section 3.***

Do you find that you use the same teaching structures (guided reading for example) again and again and again? Are you interested in finding ways to engage students in learning that isn't always teacher driven? Are you curious about how to make your teaching more responsive, even if the curriculum is set? ***Start in Section 4.***

Do you love stuff? Let's be honest, we all do. The goodies are in the back. ***Start in the appendixes.***

The world has changed, and it demands thoughtful, engaged citizens. Technology and global connectivity require collaboration and critical thinking. It is our responsibility and honor to create classrooms where students learn skills beyond the rote, that extend to their very ways of interacting with, and perhaps changing, the world. Classrooms where children learn how to make decisions, engage in thoughtful discourse, reflect, and resolve to never stop growing. So let's call on our optimism and our drive for a better world and see what we can accomplish together.

It's time to get started.

1

Teaching Is Heart Work

Introduction

We have a great teaching friend, JoEllen McCarthy (@JoEllenMcCarthy), who exudes optimism and joy. One of the things she often says is, "Teaching is heart work." But what does that mean exactly? There is a science to teaching—continuums of development, for example—but there is also an art, like the way we connect to children. Teaching without the heart is like cooking without seasoning: bland, ineffectual, and uninspiring. So how do we bring more heart into our work? By tapping into our self-compassion and ability to grow and flourish, our empathy, our spirit of play, our ability to be flexible, and our reflective selves.

The Flourishing Teacher

Welcome to Teaching: Here Is a Box of Tissues

If someone tells you teaching is easy, they probably don't really know teaching. Teaching (real, from the heart, cutting-edge, responsive teaching) is challenging, difficult work. But challenge and difficulty are the companions of words like *joyful*, *rewarding*, and *meaningful*. Teaching is for the dedicated, the passionate, the hopeful, and the innovative. But let's be honest—as with all things, our hopes outpace our skills for a long, long time. No matter where we are in our teaching career, the difference between how we envision our days with children and how those days actually play out can be kind of shocking, much like the experience of picturing the perfect date and having it go all haywire. Teaching isn't just about you putting on a magnificent one-person show; it is about the relationships and interactions of every child in the classroom. You cannot and should not plan to control all of the outcomes of your classroom; you should hope to construct them alongside your children.

The margins in this book are for your notes!

There is a pretty good chance that some of your teaching days go great. There is also a pretty good chance that some days, you want to give up. Does it help to know we all have those days? Probably not, but we all do. We have found that there are things to keep in mind (shared next) that make this journey easier on our brains and our souls and help us practice being better humans along the way.

Don't Hope for Perfection, Plan for Growth

We teachers tend to be strivers. Some of us who have prided ourselves on being the "best" students have had (and continue to have) the hardest time transitioning to being the "best" teacher. Why is that? Well, some of it is wrapped up in that word *best*. The mighty and brilliant Carol Dweck (2008, 2015, 2016a, 2016b) has done tons of research around the idea that there are two ways to describe mindsets people have. Fixed mindsets are "I am who I am" people. That is to say they believe their identity to be comprised of statements like: I am a good student, I am bad at sports, I am a good artist, I am bad at keeping secrets, I am a good daughter, and so on and so on. If this is you, then you might be wondering, *What else is my identity comprised of? Sunshine and butterflies?*

No, not exactly. Someone with a growth mindset, in the words of Carol Dweck (2016b) believes that "skills and capabilities can be developed." In other words, someone with a growth mindset would never deem themselves to be good or bad at something. Things like being a student or an artist or an athlete are neutral. You can either work at them and get better or not work at them and not develop those skills. It is a combination of belief in growth, intentional skill instruction, and an ability to see setbacks as learning opportunities that enables people with a growth mindset to outperform those with a fixed mindset (2016b).

The real key is how we see setbacks, because let's be clear, we teachers encounter a lot of them. If you see a setback as a threat to your identity ("But I am supposed to be *good* at this!"), it is very hard to confront it and learn from it. But when we are able to see setbacks as a natural part of learning and living, look at them honestly, and come away with some valuable feedback about what to try differently next time (there will always be a next time!), then we live as teachers who constantly grow and develop and constantly improve and refine our practice. Some people quit teaching because they thought it would be easy. Some people resist change or "do it how it has always been done" because they fear failing and feeling like they might be bad people. But risk and change bring a promise of growth and learning. Instead of berating yourself for mistakes, instead ask, as Carol Dweck suggests, "What are the opportunities for learning and growth today?"; "When, where, and how will I act on my plan?"; "What do I have to do to maintain and continue the growth?" (2008, 244–46).

Kristi is fifteen years into teaching at the time of this writing, and she still screws up on a weekly basis. If you are going to be constantly improving, you are going to be constantly failing. The difference is now she knows it's important to try to see failure as what it is, an opportunity for reflection and refinement of her teaching practice, not a statement of her worth as a human being.

Sometimes Taylor Swift Gives Good Advice, aka "Shake It Off": Strategies for Growth

There is no one perfect way to live as a skilled teacher, but there are some strategies that will support you as you evolve—no matter where you are along your teaching journey. Facing setbacks, shaking them off (thanks, Taylor!), and moving on is part of teaching and part of living, because learning takes time. Part of this is about commitment; you have chosen teaching as your job, which means in some regards you are imagining a good chunk of your life spent in the field. To that end, remember the teacher you are right this minute will not be the same teacher you will be in a year, or in five years, or in ten. You have chosen a craft, like woodworking or sculpting. New influences will enter your life, you will learn as you do, you will read more, understand more, shift, and change. Don't plan to figure it all out right away; let the journey be the goal.

Anchor Yourself to Beliefs

We all have a compass inside ourselves that guides our choices in life. If you believe that honesty is a critical trait, you will use that as a parameter when making choices. The same is true for teaching. If you have a series of beliefs about children and teaching, it will help you make critical decisions about teaching and will help you stick through the hard parts. It will also help you wade through the vast resources that will be thrown at you. "Does this match what I believe about children and teaching?" Sorry Shakespeare, but *that* is actually the question.

We aren't in the business of telling you what to believe, but we do want to share some beliefs that have guided our practice over the years:

⭐ Childhood is a distinct and valuable period in life. Children are not in training to be adults; they are whole and complete human beings worthy of deep respect and capable of making choices, thinking critically, and contributing to society as a whole.

⭐ Teaching should be tailored to the unique aspects of every child, and all children should feel powerful in their learning journey.

⭐ Treat children as you wish to be treated. Observe, wonder, support, and challenge. Facilitate and encourage.

⭐ Building community is a slow and powerful process that can be shortchanged when compliance and control techniques are used.

⭐ See your classroom as a microcosm of the world; ask constantly, "Is this a world I would want to live in?"

SAD SHAKESPEARE

Perhaps some of these resound with you, maybe they don't, but you need to believe something. It will change over time, expect that, but knowing what you believe maintains your integrity and your vision for what is possible. Take time and space (in the margins, in your mind) to think through your guiding beliefs.

Find a Mentor and a Community (#teachersquad)

Want to learn to swim? You don't jump into the pool and just start flailing; you find a teacher. Same is true in teaching: don't jump into a new teaching project and assume you've got it; find teachers and mentors to support you in the process. The beautiful and amazing world of technology means that your mentor does not have to be physically present in your life. They can be, which is great, but there are a myriad of other ways to find a voice of reason and aid. Twitter, Facebook, Google hangouts, and online communities can all be your support. This is helpful to know because sometimes your vision of teaching is not going to be the dominant view in your school community. You might walk into a school where the ongoing fad is to use ClassDojo, and that doesn't vibe with your belief system. Don't go it alone! Use the same apps that help you stay connected with friends to connect you with educators who will support your vision and belief system and follow people who speak your language and inspire you to be more.

Practice Self-Compassion and Positive Self-Talk: Channel Your Inner Tony Robbins

When the school year starts and we enter our classroom, whether it's for the first year or the twentieth year, it is so easy to become our own harshest critic. To have that little voice in our head turn minor failures into disasters, to hyperfocus on the negative and spiral in a vortex of gloom and doom. We've all been there. Negative self-talk and cycles of insecurity actually create neural pathways in our brains—superhighways of negativity that our autopilot brain knows all too well.

If growing and evolving as teachers means that we'll face setbacks at almost every turn, it's important that we go easy on ourselves and actively, intentionally practice self-compassion. Kristin Neff (2011) says there are three elements of self-compassion:

⭐ Self-kindness: Talk to yourself like your best friend would talk to you. Or a kind aunt or the most gentle, loving soul you can imagine. The bottom line is this: when the going gets tough, the tough need to get gentle. All of that harsh feedback won't help you thrive. Acknowledging your imperfections and being kind to yourself will calm you down, reset your brain, and help you focus on moving forward (48).

⭐ Recognition of the common human experience: Dwelling on an ideal of perfectionism or constantly comparing yourself to others only perpetuates insecurities. Instead, acknowledge that mistakes and imperfections are a part of being human (61).

⭐ Mindfulness: Be mindful of what you're experiencing; don't resist feeling pain or discomfort or hurt, but don't linger in your suffering. Suffering, according to Neff, occurs when we compare our reality to our ideals (93). Try to be aware of your reality and respond in a compassionate manner.

Go on twitter, join chats like:

#kinderchat, #1stchat, #tcrwp, #G2Great, #edchat, #educolor!

The more we practice self-compassion and positive self-talk, the more our brains rewire toward constructive, kind habits. Coming from this place of compassion prepares us to do our best teaching.

What We Live Is What We Teach

This might all feel a little gooey to you, but there is neurological research to support the basic thesis here: the more growth oriented and self-compassionate you are, the better you will get at what you are trying to do. (See Jo Boaler's work at youcubed.org for some studies.) Anchoring beliefs and supportive mentors are great, but in the absence of resilience and realistic optimism, they will feel more like a taunt than a vision. And there is a bonus to all this. In cultivating growth and self-compassion, tuning into self-talk, learning from setbacks, and seeking help and support from a community, we become better, happier people and therefore better, happier teachers. We become teachers who are not product and benchmark driven, but rather compassionate and growth minded, transmitting that very same message to our students by the way we act, the way we talk, and the choices we make in the small moments when we think they aren't watching.

NOTICING THIS?

Your perfectly planned lessons keep going haywire.

INSTEAD OF...

Feeling defeated and thinking that all of your great ideas and hopes and visions are pointless

TRY THIS...

Self-talk yourself to a better place. Think of another time when you learned something incredibly complex; remind yourself that over time, with support, you learned those skills. Make that a model for your teaching years.

Then, reflect. What exactly is going haywire? What theories do you have about why? Who do you know and respect who can help you come up with strategies to change the dynamic?

The Empathetic Teacher

What exactly is empathy, you might ask? It's not sympathy, and it's not compassion. It is something unique: the ability to see the world from another person's perspective and to understand and feel what that person feels in the moment. The other people in this case? Your students. Empathy isn't just feeling *for*, it is feeling *like*, meaning you can honestly get inside the head and feelings of a five-year-old, a ten-year-old, a twelve-year-old. You might think that being an empathetic teacher is just part of the gig ("Of *course* I'm going have empathy for my students—I care about them, I'm a kind person, I'm a teacher for crying out loud!"), but in the heat of the moment and the stress of the job, it is easy to want kids to see it from our point of view ("I'm trying to teach you! Listen!") rather than to see it from theirs ("We've been sitting for a long time and we need to move!"). Yes, empathy is a feel-good idea, but there's more to it than that.

John Hattie and Gregory Yates, preeminent educational researchers, have studied the effect size of certain teaching "mind frames" and found that the more connected you are to your students, the more empathetic you are as a teacher, and the better your students will do: "Learning for many students is risky business. The positive student-teacher relationship is thus important . . . because it helps build the trust to make mistakes, to ask for help, to build confidence to try again, and for students to know they will not look silly when they don't get it the first time" (Hattie and Yates 2013, 21). The relationships you form with your students provide the safe and sturdy foundation for all other learning to come, and the empathy you model sends a powerful message about how we treat each other in the world.

Keep a Child's-Eye View of Your Day

Every time you structure your day or plan a lesson, put yourself in your students' shoes. How does it feel from their perspective? Sometimes it can be hard as a teacher to see things from our students' perspectives. Think back to when you were the age of the children you teach. Try to call up memories of being six or eight or ten. Sometimes children and adults perceive the same things very differently. Have you ever noticed how so many children are drawn to walking on the tops of walls? To children, these walls look like the perfect, adventurous route to wherever you might be going. To adults, they might look too wobbly, too tall, too narrow, too out of the way. When you think about your day and your space, try to be mindful of the unique needs of your group of children, and change things up if you need to. For much more on being a responsive teacher, see Section 4.

 Time: How would this amount of time feel to the children in my class? Does this seem like it is within the reach of their stamina?

 Choice: What are the children's choices in this? Can I give them any more choice or flexibility?

 Materials/Space: What materials am I presenting to children? Are they engaging, size-appropriate, and useful? What about the space? Is it conducive to all students' needs?

 Agency: Does this lesson/activity/material give power or take power from children? Does this lead to active problem solving or passive response?

 Independence: Is this something I am doing for a child, or something the child can do for him- or herself? Can I do less so the child can do more?

 Relevance: How does this connect to what the children already know, wonder about, love?

 Willpower/Energy: How much energy will children have to expend? Can I add in more unstructured elements so children are not just following rules and directions, but instead thinking and problem solving?

The Empathy Toolkit

No matter what the situation, we activate our empathy and are more compassionate and effective if we follow Theresa Wiseman's (1996) "four attributes of empathy":

For more on especially tricky moments, see "Supporting Every Child" on page 93 and for more on introducing the idea of empathy to your class, check out Kristi and Christine's book *A Mindset for Learning: Teaching the Traits of Joyful, Independent Growth* (2015).

Take their *perspective*. Put yourself in your student's shoes and use your whole body to show that you're empathizing. Get down on their level. Turn your body and your full attention to their concern. Imagine, really imagine in your brain what it would be like to be in their position.

Don't rush to *judgment*. What might be seen as a trivial problem to us as adults may just mean the world to a five-, seven-, or ten-year-old. Catch yourself if you're rushing to judgment or rushing to dismiss what they're upset about. Instead of sympathizing or fixing or negating the problem, just listen and let them be heard.

Recognize *emotions*. Try to home in on the emotions that the student is expressing or attempting to communicate. To do this, you'll have to put aside your own emotions. Helping your student to name the emotion that they're feeling is one of the first steps to calming them down and tapping into their reasoning brains.

Communicate and *connect*. Brené Brown (2012) says that the two most important words when you're trying to be empathetic, when you're trying to reach someone who is struggling, are "Me too." Try to connect with a student and communicate your understanding of what they're going through. To do this, you might have to put aside your desire to get things done, keep things moving, and have a neat and tidy teaching moment. But even the best-made plans are worth putting aside to connect, to really connect, with a student.

NOTICING THIS?

It is hard to connect to your students and have an empathetic response during difficult moments.

INSTEAD OF...

Getting down on yourself and seeing only the times you're not being empathetic

TRY THIS...

Make it as easy for yourself as you can. Keep a sticky note close at hand with the key phrases of an empathetic response:

"I'm listening." "Tell me more about that."
"It sounds like you're feeling. . ." "Me too."

The more you practice an empathetic response, the faster it will become a habit and your natural response to children who are having a difficult time.

The Playful Teacher

Make a Pla(y)ce for Play

Truth talk: teaching is hard and it is work. We get tired, we get sweaty, and we get frustrated. It happens to all of us. Yet, here is the thing: we have our best days when we hold on to a spirit of play. What does that mean exactly? It means that as teachers we are joyful, willing to improvise, willing to laugh. It means we don't expect children to be miniature adults, and we know that there is as much learning in playing with blocks as there is in a math lesson. Play is a natural right for children, but it is also an essential one for us, as their teachers. Understanding child development is serious business, but teaching isn't; teaching is about ensuring a joyful, challenging journey for each child. How can we do that if we do not remain joyful and challenged ourselves?

Incorporating play and movement into your classroom is essential and will be addressed in later chapters. This section is about incorporating play within yourself. It doesn't just increase happiness, but it also increases our brain function. As a matter of fact, Stuart Brown, one of the authors of *Play* (Brown and Vaughan 2010), writes, "Play seems to be one of the most advanced methods nature has invented to allow a complex brain to invent itself" (39). For children and adults, a playful mindset allows us to face difficulty with optimism, develop unique new ideas, and find joy in all tasks.

It is hard to define what makes something play exactly, but Brown has found that there are very distinct ways people like to play. He calls them play personalities—and understanding your play personality can help you infuse it into all your days, bringing joy to even the days when you just want to cry. Identifying your play personalities is as simple as identifying the things that bring you the most pleasure, when you seem to lose time and you can feel your creative juices flowing. You will likely find yourself reflected in more than one category! The goal is that we pay attention to ourselves and the things that bring us joy. (Check out pages 14–15 for specifics on the play personalities.)

Tapping into Your Play Personalities

Kristi identifies primarily as a storyteller (with some joker and competitor woven in) and brings that into her classroom by crafting stories for even the most mundane tasks. Day-dreaming about other worlds on the subway ride means she enters her classroom smiling. On a day when everyone in the classroom has high spirits, she helps the class reimagine the walk to art as a moon walk. Christine, who at her core is equal parts explorer and creator, walks into the classroom every day brimming with questions, curiosities, and ideas about how to best engage and support her students. When her second-grade students want to produce a Star Wars movie, Christine guides them in gathering materials, writing a script, creating the set, and shooting the scenes. Being a playful teacher means that you understand joy and laughter means more thinking and neural networking is happening, not less. Being a playful teacher means that you know being happy is no little thing, and it is part of our job description.

Knowing your play personality also allows you to identify and empathize with your children's very powerful human drive to play. They, like you, need play to feel happy, safe, and challenged. Resist punishing playful behaviors, and instead see the opportunity for powerful joyful work inherent in them. What seems like a child interrupting your lesson with noises might be a joker's personality trying to connect with others. A wiggling, moving, jumping, touching, out-of-his-seat child could be a kinesthete looking for an outlet. This isn't meant to be disruptive or upsetting to you; this is a child bringing play and his identity into the class-room. Punishing it sends a message of exclusion and judgment; finding a reasonable outlet sends a message of inclusion and worth. Identifying the fact that a child loves to move allows you to rework that child's school experience so it incorporates more movement—setting her up to sit on a rocking chair, for example. Seeing the joy a child has in collecting things means you understand why that child wants to read every book in a series before moving on. Seeing the explorer on the playground might help you engage a writer through a spirit of inquiry and discovery. The playful teacher is the one who honors play's power in all its forms and nourishes it in herself and in her children.

The hardest day is the one when we lose our sense of play. Here are resources to help you learn more:

- *Play: How It Shapes the Brain, Opens the Imagination, and Invigorates the Soul* by Dr. Stuart Brown and Christopher Vaughan (2010)

- *Purposeful Play: A Teacher's Guide to Igniting Deep and Joyful Learning Across the Day* by Kristine Mraz, Alison Porcelli, and Cheryl Tyler (2016)

- *Choice Time: How to Deepen Learning Through Inquiry and Play, PreK–2* by Renée Dinnerstein (2016)

- *A Quick Guide to Boosting English Acquisition in Choice Time, K–2* by Alison Porcelli and Cheryl Tyler (2008)

- *Working in the Reggio Way: A Beginner's Guide for American Teachers* by Julianne Wurm (2005)

NOTICING THIS?
You're completely sapped of energy after a hard day.

INSTEAD OF...
Replaying what went wrong and getting trapped in a spiral of negativity

TRY THIS...
A happier you makes for a happier classroom. Think about your play personality and what you can do between now and the next day to bring some joy into your own life.

Stuart Brown's

	JOKER	KINESTHETE	EXPLORER	COMPETITOR
PLAY PERSONALITY				
DESCRIPTION	Jokers love to make people laugh, or just laughing themselves. Their play "always revolves around some kind of nonsense" (2010, 66).	These players "find themselves happiest moving" (2010, 66). These aren't just athletes, either; they can be people who think best when walking, or just enjoy the feel of movement.	The explorers love discovering new things: mental, physical, and emotional (2010, 67).	These players love to turn everything into a game, and to win! (2010, 67).
IN THE CLASSROOM	Tap into your personality by using dramatic voices to engage children, laughing with them, embracing silliest of situations, and honoring their desires to make people laugh. Remember the ridiculous things to help you through a hard moment.	Incorporate your love of movement into your teaching with dance, yoga, flexible seating options, and plenty of space for big movement. Need a moment to collect yourself? Go for a walk or dance with the door closed.	Engage with your students over a shared sense of wonder. Explore the community around your school and the wider world with inquiry projects and your deep spirit of curiosity. Keep yourself engaged as a teacher by exploring new ideas in teaching and in yourself.	Turn your love of challenge and drive to win toward your teaching practice by creating a game out of even the most unremarkable tasks, strategizing about what teaching moves would be most effective, and (always) encouraging good sportsmanship. Tired of paperwork? Make it a game to get it done.

Play Personalities

DIRECTOR

"Directors enjoy planning and executing scenes and events" (2010, 67).

Use your love of organizing and planning to orchestrate special events, units, and experiences for your class. Be transparent in what you do and invite your students to plan and direct right alongside you. Share your love of planning so the directors in your class have time to shine too.

COLLECTOR

Collectors enjoy the act of gathering, collating, organizing, and admiring objects and experiences (2010, 68).

Focus your passion for collecting on your classroom community. Document the year in photographs, curate a treasury of beloved stories, support your students in keeping portfolios of their work.

ARTIST/CREATOR

For the artists, "joy is found in making things" (2010, 68).

Carve out time to make things not just *for* but *with* your students. Co-construct bulletin boards, teach your students new art habits and practices just like you would writing lessons or math strategies, and follow wherever their creative or artistic interests lead.

STORYTELLER

Storytellers use their imagination in all things, and also love reading and watching movies (2010, 69).

Leverage your love of story to bring play and imagination into every area of your teaching. Use your vivid ability to storytell to see multiple solutions to problems and to engage your students in their learning. Take time to read and dream in your busy day.

The Flexible Teacher

Balancing Act

Sometimes when we enter new teaching situations, we grip what we know with an iron will, but flexibility is key to success in teaching. Add to that the fact that almost all teachers are asked, at some point, to teach certain standards in a certain way at a certain time of the school year, and it can feel like there is only one route to take in your classroom. If you are a brand-new teacher, you might have left your first week of inservice with sets of curricula for math, reading, writing, word study, science, and social studies stuffed into your teacher tote bag and a head spinning with questions. And we all know that new things are always being added to our teaching plates, every year—forget last year's math curriculum, this year we're doing *this* one! One of the biggest balancing acts of teaching is finding ways to be flexible in the often inflexible context in which you've found yourself. It's not hard to fear that being flexible will lead you astray from what you need to do. You know you *must* teach what's expected, but it is important to weave in your own style of teaching and stay true to your anchoring beliefs. How can that happen? And what about the interests, passions, and needs all of the students in front of you? How can you balance it all? First, take a breath—this gets easier; next, take a close look at exactly what is and what is not in your control. There is often more wiggle room than might first appear. Then, find your flexibility and run with it!

What Is Always in Your Control?

⭐ Your classroom environment: Even if you can't pick out the nicest furniture, what you bring into your classroom, how you arrange your furniture, and what you put on your walls (or don't!) are largely under your control. Let your space reflect your beliefs about teaching and, most importantly, your children and your class. For much more on your classroom environment, see Section 2.

⭐ Your relationships with children: When all else fails, fall back on really, truly getting to know and connecting with your children. This foundation of compassion, understanding, and empathy should be the basis for every aspect of your teaching.

⭐ Your spirit of joy and play: Find ways to bring humor, story, and laughter into the seemingly most mundane lessons or procedures by remembering that, above all else, you teach children!

How Can You Be Flexible?

CAN YOU MODIFY THE TIME?

- Tweak something in the scope and sequence you teach to better fit your students' needs.
- Change up the amount of time you devote to a given lesson—sometimes this means zooming through material and sometimes this means lingering with the same lesson for a few days.
- For example: Mollie knew that her children were skilled narrative writers based on reading their work. She shortened her narrative writing unit by a week to build in a week of independent writing projects.
- For more on modifying time, see "Scheduling for Success" on page 60.

CAN YOU MODIFY THE TEACHING STRUCTURE?

- Try different teaching structures such as whole-group, small-group, or one-on-one conferences depending on exactly which students need a given lesson.
- Determine if guided practice, demonstration, or inquiry would best fit the situation.
- For example: Chris decided not to tell his first-grade students what kinds of eggs they were hatching like the other teachers on his grade team had done. Instead, he brought in pictures and books and had the children build theories and debate the possibilities.
- For more on different teaching structures, see page 118.

CAN YOU MODIFY TO BRING IN YOUR STUDENTS' INTERESTS?

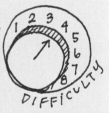

- Give students choice—about math problems, books they're reading, writing topics, everything!—as much as possible.
- Notice that most of the class is obsessed with Star Wars/Minecraft/Pokemon/the Olympics? Incorporate those interests in your lessons as much as you can.
- For example: Anna noticed her children's obsession with Minecraft so she borrowed books on the topic from the library for independent reading, and crafted math lessons using the principles of the game.
- For more on being responsive to your students, see page 108.

CAN YOU MODIFY THE DEGREE OF DIFFICULTY?

- Differentiate your teaching based on what your students really need. Find ways to reinforce the lesson for students who need more support and extend the lesson for students who need more challenge. Don't be worried if this seems challenging—it's one of the hardest parts of teaching, and we have much more on differentiation in Section 4.
- For example: Jack knew his math lesson on solving story problems used large numbers. He created three versions for independent practice so that children could practice the skill (solving story problems) on numbers within their comfort level.

CAN YOU MODIFY THE MATERIALS?

- Think about what materials would really engage and thrill your students. Think nice pens for writing, whiteboard and erasers for math, up-to-date books for guided reading, and do your best to bring them into your classroom.
- Create materials (charts, personal word walls, visual schedules) that give students something to refer back to.
- For example: Mira made a new alphabet chart for her students based on vocabulary they knew and loved.

TIP!

Be sure to back up your decisions with information (data!) from observations and assessments and research. Be ready to justify your teaching moves if anyone asks why. For much more on being a responsive teacher, see Section 4.

NOTICING THIS?

Your school asks you to implement a program or practice that doesn't fit with your beliefs about education.

INSTEAD OF...

Getting all up in arms and voicing your outrage at the first team meeting or simply refusing to follow the school/district/nation's expectations

TRY THIS...

Start by assuming that everyone has children's best interests at heart and ask questions:

How long has the school or grade had this practice? Where did the practice come from? What goal is the school trying to meet?

The more questions you ask, the more you'll understand the motivation behind the practice and you'll be better equipped to offer an alternative or advocate for your students' specific needs.

The Reflective Teacher

Before we dig into this section, a quick note. We cannot possibly convey the enormity of bias and the critical need to battle it within a few pages. However, we can't ignore it either. Our hope is that if you are just beginning to think about bias, this will open further conversations and resources for you, and if you have spent a lifetime battling bias, we honor the work you do each and every day.

I've Got Bias, Yes I Do. I've Got Bias, How 'Bout You?

Several years ago, Kristi was at a workshop with Carl Anderson, guru of all things writing, when he said something about how he always found it easier to confer with kids writing about baking with Gramma than kids writing about vomiting cats, but that he has since learned each story carries equal value *to the child* and therefore needs to carry equal value with the *teacher*. This got Kristi thinking deeply about the way her teaching carried all sorts of messages of value and preference—from how she chose her read-alouds to how she responded to children's work. Did she do it from the assumption that all stories, literally and figuratively, have equal value?

This brings us to the idea of bias. We all carry bias in us; you can't be human and not have some sort of preference for one thing over another. If a Kmart and a Target are next to each other, Christine is always going to go to the Target. This isn't necessarily a logical choice, nor always a wise one, but she is biased toward the design aesthetic of Target, the layout of the store, the packaging, and the ad campaigns. This bias seems innocuous enough until you consider what this would mean if she had a lot of power suddenly. What if Christine decreed all stores had to be Target? Not because it has better prices or fairer hiring practices, but because she likes it more. What does that mean for the rest of the world? There are many problems with bias, not the least of which is operating as though our bias is a fact, therefore never questioned. In our classrooms, where we wield tremendous power, our unexamined bias can have devastating consequences. As we begin to reflect on our own biases, keep in mind that this is complex work, and remember that it is OK—necessary, really—to start with small steps, as long as you start.

A Fascinating Excursion into a Real-Life Example of Unconscious Bias in Action

Walter Gilliam, a researcher at Yale, wanted to explore people's implicit bias. You can't tell people you want to study their implicit bias because it no longer is implicit, and they become acutely aware of the choices they make. So, here is what his team did. They rounded up some pre-K teachers and asked them to watch a video so they could analyze how teachers "detect challenging behavior" (Gilliam et al. 2016, 6). They gave them a video to watch featuring four pre-K students, a black boy, a black girl, a white boy, and a white girl, and asked them to hit a certain key every time they saw "a behavior that could become a potential challenge" (6). In short, identify trouble before it starts—something teachers try to do all day long.

There were two tricks to the study. The first was that there *was* no challenging behavior displayed in the video, so the teachers were watching with a lens that did not actually correlate with the events unfolding. The second was that the researchers were actually watching the teacher's eyes. Who did the teacher watch when they heard there was going to be challenging behavior? From the article:

> "What we found was exactly what we expected based on the rates at which children are expelled from preschool programs," Gilliam says. "Teachers looked more at the black children than the white children, and they looked specifically more at the African-American boy."
>
> Indeed, according to recent data from the U.S. Department of Education, black children are 3.6 times more likely to be suspended from preschool than white children. Put another way, black children account for roughly 19 percent of all preschoolers, but nearly half of preschoolers who get suspended.
>
> One reason that number is so high, Gilliam suggests, is that teachers spend more time focused on their black students, expecting bad behavior. "If you look for something in one place, that's the only place you can typically find it" (NPREd 2016).

The thing is, most of us want to believe that we would have been fair and equitable if we had participated in that study, but the honest truth is, we probably would have been just like every other teacher who participated. But now that we know that, we can do something about it. Having bias is like needing glasses, but not realizing it. Once we get an eye exam, and see how different the world looks when calibrated with others, we notice when the world becomes blurry again.

Examining Bias: When You Know Better, You Can Do Better

How many of these statements have you heard, or maybe even thought?

Girls are better readers and writers.

Boys are more rambunctious.

City children are more disadvantaged.

"Regular" classwork is too hard for kids with disabilities.

Now think: Where did you first hear them? How did you come to maybe even hold some of these ideas yourself? What other statements could you add to this list? All of these point to some level of bias. Bias, as defined in the book *Anti-Bias Education for Young Children and Ourselves*, is "an attitude, belief, or feeling that helps to justify unfair treatment because of his or her identity" (Derman-Sparks and Edwards 2009, xi). Think of these statements in view of that definition of bias. How do we treat boys unfairly because we are biased to find them more rambunctious? How do we justify unfair treatment of children with disabilities because we assume they cannot do certain things?

Our feelings and attitudes toward people of color; lesbian, gay, bisexual, queer, and transgender people; people from social classes different from our own; people of different or unassigned genders; people with disabilities, and so on, permeate everything we do, unless we learn to stop assuming our thoughts and feelings are truth and instead start examining them. (See our interview with Jessica Lifshitz on page 25 for some ways to do that.)

First and foremost, accept this fact: we all have bias. Even if you don't want to have bias, you have bias. If you think *skin color does not matter*, that is its own kind of bias. Kristi and Christine have bias. You have bias. The teacher next to you has bias. The bus driver has bias.

Now this one: Our bias affects everyone around us if it remains unexamined and unquestioned. We called this section "The Reflective Teacher," because our ability to reflect is going to be key in our ability to be powerful teachers for all kids and a better human being in general.

Battling Bias in the Classroom

OK, so we have all accepted we are flawed human beings, but maybe we are thinking things like, *But I am not* that *bad. I would never discriminate against a child who was a different race than me.* But the thing is overt racism is just one way that bias manifests. Sometimes overt action is an easier form of bias to see and address in classrooms. It's the more passive, subtle, and commonplace choices being made that we don't always notice. In their book *Anti-Bias Education for Young Children and Ourselves,* authors Louise Derman-Sparks and Julie Olsen Edwards talk about the importance of overt and covert messages that children receive. They describe overt messages as those that are "explicitly declared" like "Be careful. She's a girl. She can get hurt" (2009, 13). But children receive just as much information in the covert messages they receive or "indirect messages . . . tiny or unseen messages that accumulate over time to create harm" (13). These may run counter to, and therefore undermine, some of the overt messages we try to send. If in our classroom we say, "Families can look many different ways" and then we only read books that represent one kind of family, our overt message of sameness overwhelms and undermines our covert message of diversity as fact. Likewise, if we react differently to a boy who gets hurt ("Shake it off") than to a girl who gets hurt ("Oh, honey, are you OK? That was a scary fall!"), we inadvertently reinforce gender stereotypes that we may overtly deny.

Our knee-jerk reactions seem to display more deeply held beliefs and bias than our well-constructed words. Analyze what you do in the heat of the moment to find the flaws in what you might believe to be true about kids and the world.

Baby Steps to a Better World

Fighting bias, our own and others', is not a one-day event. Much like your growth mindset, and your flexibility, and your playfulness, your willingness to address and confront your own bias is a daily activity. We will invariably make mistakes and missteps, but that is to be expected as we try to confront our own bias. It is our capacity to reflect honestly and openly about ourselves and our actions that allows us to grow and keep growing as people. Just as we transmit attitudes about failure and challenge to our students, we can transmit ideas of bias or critical thinking and reflective living. Small actions can yield big results in our classrooms.

Visibility Versus Invisibility

Take every book that has a family in it in your classroom library out and sort the books into piles of what kind of family they show. Even if the family is not the point of the story, the illustrations or mentions of the family still get filed into covert messages children receive. Whether the characters are humans or animals, you are going to find one pile growing much higher and much faster than any other, that of the mom/dad/kids variety, likely middle-class homeowners. (Authors' note: At one point we had the word *typical* in here, until we realized that, in itself was biased—so a family with one parent or two moms is abnormal? No! Hence, the edit of the word *typical*.) This is an institutional and systemic problem, a publishing problem, and a cultural problem. It is also an identity problem for young children. From *Anti-Bias Education for Young Children and Ourselves*, "When children see themselves and their families reflected in their early childhood setting, they feel affirmed and that they belong. When children's identities and families are invisible, the opposite happens" (Derman-Sparks and Edwards 2009, 13). Have you ever been in a place where you were the only one like you? How daunting, and scary, and intimidating was that? For some children, that is their entire schooling experience. A child who has two dads, or a single parent, or is being raised by a grandparent, will not read *Chrysanthemum* (Henkes 2008) and see their supportive mom and dad and connect to their own experience. And they don't look at Henry and Mudge and see their own lives represented in the suburban middle-class setting. They don't see heroes who look and act like them. The materials in your classroom should represent every child in your room, and open possibilities for lives other than ones they know. Setting up a classroom library, curating materials for lessons, and bringing in materials for play are all ethical and political issues; don't treat them lightly, treat them as catalysts for change.

Look Beyond the Single Story

Chad Everett, in his interview for this book on page 29, talks about being mindful of quantity versus quality of materials. All "diverse" books are not created equal. As a matter of fact, many books that tout diversity actually reinforce stereotypes. Chimamanda Ngozi Adichie, in her incredible TED talk "The Danger of a Single Story" (2009), discusses how we can inadvertently use one narrative to categorize an entire people, in her case being treated by others with the assumption that all people from Africa are poor and come from drought-ridden, desolate lands. When we look back at our piles of books about families, when we look at one of the piles that is not the dominant narrative, like one with a single dad, or single mom, is the same story being told in each book? The varieties of experience are too rich and nuanced to ever capture within the confines of a single story. All single dads aren't bad at doing their daughters' hair; all single moms are not struggling to make ends meet because of a deadbeat dad.

This can start to feel daunting. Not only is it bigger than just having books that make many experiences visible, but it's about having books that do that in rich and nuanced ways. These books and materials don't yet exist to the degree that they are needed in our classrooms, but even if they did, the real work is about how we teach children to consume these materials with questions in mind. Chad covers more of that in his interview.

Echo and Amplify, aka, Make Space for Another Voice

One of the most important things we can do to make change is to understand our position in the power hierarchy. Some people, because of race, wealth, or other societal privileges, have an easier time getting their voice out there. If you are someone who has power, the goal is not to speak for others, but to "echo and amplify" those with more marginalized voices. What does that mean? At a staff conference, you might invite the voice of a colleague who does not often get their ideas shared. In the classroom, you might set a model for ensuring even the quietest voices have a space and a way to share. And in the world? In the world it means giving space and time to the voices most often overlooked. It would be beyond hypocritical at this point to act as though we invented these ideas. So, let us direct you to the brilliant professionals who have made the topics of race, bias, and inclusion the basis of their study and their work.

Stop reading, get to the computer, and find and follow these powerful voices:

Rusul Alrubail
https://rusulalrubail.com/about/

Ebony Elizabeth Thomas
http://scholar.gse.upenn.edu/thomas

Laura Jimenez
https://booktoss.wordpress.com

Debbie Reese
http://americanindiansinchildrensliterature.net

Jose Vilson
http://thejosevilson.com

Cornelius Minor
@misterminor

As well as these resources:

Zinn Ed Project
https://zinnedproject.org

Teaching Tolerance
www.tolerance.org

#educolor on Twitter

If you are a person who has power because society has deemed it so, you will read things that make you uncomfortable. Don't stop reading. Discomfort can be the first step of deep and powerful change.

Conclusion: Glad We Got That All Figured Out

Ah, if only. The only way, it seems, to be a really powerful and impactful teacher is to first be a vulnerable and flawed human. When we walk into a classroom, sometimes the advice is to arm ourselves in layers of protection. Don't smile, don't look weak, never go back on a decision once you have made it. Yet, in our experience, all of those scraps of "wisdom" perpetuate and create the sort of schooling we seek to subvert. We are cultivating citizens, humanitarians, change makers. We are contributing to critical, curious thinking. We are advocating for kindness and empathy. We create better worlds by making ourselves better. We advocate wrapping yourself in layers of joy and playfulness, in the capacity to reflect honestly and make change when you see yourself acting in biased or inflexible ways; we suggest you aim to grow, not "win," at teaching. With every page you turn in this book, see it from the lens of joy and growth, antibias, and truly flexible thinking, and know that the revolution for a better world begins with your classroom. You are the change. We are the change.

Jessica Lifshitz is a teacher in Illinois. You can find more of her work on her blog crawlingoutoftheclassroom.wordpress.com or on Twitter (@Jess5th). We asked Jess about how teachers can identify and address our own biases.

Q Can you tell us a little about how you keep your own biases in mind when you're teaching?

A Being aware of my own biases is something that is fairly new to me. A few years ago, I would have told you that I did not have any biases. And I truly believed that was the truth. Over the course of the past few years, I have learned from the brilliance of others and have been able to look at my own biases and recognize how much they impact me and the way I interact with the world.

One of the best things that I have learned to do is to notice when people are presented in just one way. If there is a group of people and they all look alike, I now notice that and question why that is and then see what I can do to make sure that a larger variety of people and experiences are represented. This could be when looking at characters in books or at the people presented as examples within our curriculum.

Something else that I try to do is catch myself making assumptions. I have truly had to work to change my patterns of thinking, and one way I can do this is by interrupting the things that used to be automatic. So when I see a student, if I notice myself making an assumption that the student must be struggling, I really question if that is because I have *seen* the student struggle or because I am assuming they are struggling. And then I push myself to dig deeper and not rest on those assumptions.

Q Can you give an example of assuming struggle rather than seeing it?

A When a student comes to me with a label of an "English learner," I can sometimes let that label and the assumptions that I make about that student because he or she has a label lead me before my own observations of that student. For example, if a child with an EL label gives up on multiple books, I might assume that she is giving up because the books are too hard and she does not understand the words. I might then recommend only easy books, and assume that the struggle is because the student is finding the text level too challenging. However, that might not be the problem at all. If I can, instead, have a conversation with the student and *ask* that student what the problem is, I might find out that she is abandoning books because there is not enough action or not enough emotion or because the genre is one that she is not enjoying or because she is lacking schema on that book. Then I can recommend books that deal with that specific problem. Then, I am basing my teaching moves on actual information that I have gathered on the child sitting next to me and not based on my assumptions about an entire group of children.

Q What if I work with people who are totally unaware of their own biases? What can I do to start a conversation?

A I think the very best thing that we can do is make ourselves vulnerable by sharing our own biases with others. I find that this works with other adults and also with our own students. They will not feel comfortable sharing their biases

if I have not shared my own. The other thing that I think is important is to move away from the idea that only bad people hold racist biases. I think that we can do this by looking at how our own biases are most often products of our environments. We have grown up surrounded by biased images that present entire groups of people in only one way. We cannot help but absorb these ideas into our ways of thinking. We can talk about the single stories that are told about groups of people and then discuss ways that they impact the way that we think. This makes it easier to accept that we will all hold these biases. Having biases does not make someone a bad person; however, refusing to acknowledge your own biases and work to move past them, that becomes problematic.

Q Do you also talk about systemic bias? And how people benefit from it or are harmed by it?

A Systemic racism and bias is such a difficult concept for kids to grasp. Again, it is so hard for them to see things at a systems level. So instead of using the words *systemic bias* or *systemic racism*, we focus on patterns and trends that we see in the world around us, and then we work backward to think about the reasons that these patterns and trends might exist. I want to introduce to them the idea that when a group of people struggles with similar issues, it cannot be because something is different with that group of people, but instead we need to look at what conditions has this group of people been subjected to that have led to the current struggles people might be experiencing. Starting to prompt fifth graders to think this way can help form the foundations for them to really dig into the idea of systemic bias.

Q What are the most important things a teacher can do to make sure the future is a more empathic and justice-oriented one?

A I think we need to broaden our idea of what it means to teach. For too long, we have taught our students how to simply be better readers, better writers, better mathematicians, and better scientists. Instead, I think that we need to be teaching our students how to use reading, writing, math, and science to go out and make the world a better place. How do we do this? I think it starts by looking at what we have to teach, the standards we have to cover, and thinking about how can we work these into the kind of work that we want our students to be doing in the world outside of our classroom.

I also think we need to stop trying to protect our students from the problems of the world and instead start following our students into looking more closely at the problems that matter to them. We are lucky; we work with children. Children are these incredibly naturally empathetic and curious beings. We work so hard to shield them from anything unpleasant, but their natural sense of justice makes the very things that we are shielding them from the things that they most want to learn about. By picking up on what our children are saying and asking, we will know what they are ready to handle. Then we just need to follow them into that work.

"I think that we need to be teaching our students how to use reading, writing, math, and science to go out and make the world a better place."

Sara Ahmed is teacher, literacy coach, and writer. You can find more of her work in the book *Upstanders: How to Engage Middle School Hearts and Minds with Inquiry*, with Harvey Daniels (2014), her upcoming book *Being the Change: Lessons and Strategies to Teach Social Comprehension* (2018), and on Twitter (@SaraKAhmed). We asked Sara about how teachers can help students develop their self-identity and inclusivity.

Q Can you start by defining the concept of self-identity?

A How do you see yourself? How do others see you? How does that inform the way you understand the world?

Identity work/study of one's identity is a foundational understanding of the self within the world around us. The way we react to our environment(s), whether familiar or unfamiliar—our sensory response is grounded in our self-identity. We must first examine, reflect, question, read, write, and pause to hold up the mirror. Then we have a more honest lens to see outside of ourselves.

Q Can you tell us a little about why it's important for students to develop their self-identities?

A Kids are constantly growing through patterns of physical, social, linguistic, and cognitive change. They experience such rapid and sporadic transitions in their lives. Without even knowing, they are in a state of perpetual self-exploration. Kids need time and space to experiment, play, take risks, wonder, socialize, and explore as a means to developing a healthy sense of identity. If we can support them in developmentally appropriate ways, they will also develop a strong sense of empathy. The road to empathy leads through self-identity. We can never ask them to put themselves in someone else's shoes if they haven't yet developed a sense of what it is like to be in their own shoes first.

Q What are some of the most effective ways for teachers to initiate this work in their classrooms?

A Identity webs, as mentioned in our book *Upstanders*, are great starting point with all learners. Images, home language, digital—are all types of identity webs. Working closely with families; so much of what students carry with them comes from home. No matter the size, their "self-identity backpacks" are packed full of experience, family, language, home culture, and so much more.

To ground it all in what is familiar to the students first, and that is themselves. Naming any one piece of your identity and finding a connection, question, or path to understanding to a difficult and relevant topic is key. (Example for me: as a woman of color, I am connecting _____ or as the daughter of immigrants, I am feeling a certain way that others may not, and that is OK.)

There is so much recommended reading. But for starters, read the work of Sonia Nieto and Paulo Freire, Alfie Kohn, Dr. Beverly Daniel Tatum, Dr. Terrence Roberts, Julia Alvarez, and Jhumpa Lahiri. Chip Wood's *Yardsticks* is a great book to understand development at every age, academically and socially.

But again, whatever you are asking of your students, try yourself first. The same way you wouldn't read a book with them before reading it yourself.

Listen. Listen to and watch your kids. Kid watching yields tremendous information on how kids can interact with each other, how they may approach difficult conversations, and how they see themselves. Be an expert observer of your kids. It helps them develop that healthy sense of self when they know someone is listening to them as well.

Q What are the most important things a teacher can do to make sure the future is a more empathic and justice-oriented one?

A First and foremost: never forget why you made the choice to teach.

Follow your gut. Remember that the Common Core/any state standards are a document. Do not ask them for permission. There is no document that will ever replace the critical love and commitment of a teacher. Teachers are the experts in the room, on the ground with our kids, who know the world is better when we raise empathic students in justice-oriented classrooms.

Be a student of your own identity and bias: How do you see yourself? How do others see you? How does that two-way examination inform your bias in the world and in the classroom?

Chad Everett is a teacher and consultant in Horn Lake, Mississippi. You can find more of his thinking and work on Twitter (@chadceverett). We asked Chad about how teachers can critically analyze the materials we use in our classrooms.

Q What does *diversity* mean to you? What do most people get wrong when they talk about representing or teaching diversity in classrooms?

A To me, diversity is both quantitative and qualitative; however, I feel as though we often only look at the quantitative side. For example, when evaluating our classroom libraries, we tend to look at the number of books we have representing diverse lives, but we do not always evaluate the quality of those representations. Some representations reinforce stereotypes and myths. Put another way, a seat at the table is nice, but it means nothing if I can't eat (i.e., have my voice heard and valued).

Q What are questions I can ask myself when looking at materials or curriculum?

A These questions came from personal communication with Dana Stachowiak. [Dana Stachowiak, Ph.D., is an expert in social justice and diversity education and well versed in using literacy best practices to build teacher and student empowerment. She is currently Assistant Professor of Curriculum and Instruction in the Watson College of Education at the University of North Carolina Wilmington.] You can find more in the book *Culturally Affirming Literacy Practices for Urban Elementary Students*, edited by Lakia M. Scott and Barbara Purdum-Cassidy (2016).

- ★ What is the knowledge claim that the author is trying to make?
- ★ Who benefits from or is limited by that knowledge claim?
- ★ Who/What does the knowledge claim give power to?
- ★ What stereotypes/biases/myths are challenged/upheld?
- ★ At what points do you notice yourself resisting the book, the characters, or the author?
- ★ What does your resistance say about the book, and what does it say about you?
- ★ How does this book help you think about social issues you care about or causes you are committed to?

For more, read:

- Rudine Sims Bishop
- Pedro Noguera
- Lisa Delpit
- Chris Emdin

And check out:

- Teaching Tolerance (TT is excellent for a variety of resources on justice, equity, and diversity— including resources for examining classroom libraries with students.)
- Educolor
- We Need Diverse Books
- Donalyn Miller (curates a nice list of awards that recognize diverse books).

Q What if I am in a community that is not comfortable talking about issues of race, poverty, sexual orientation, and basically anything that can make people feel uncomfortable? How can I begin (and sustain) these conversations?

A To this I would respond, "What if I were in a community or school not comfortable talking about best practices in reading and writing?" As long as we continue to view these conversations/topics as peripheral—not essential—we won't make the progress we are striving to achieve. Heck, I work in Mississippi. I'm cognizant of my location, but I do my best to avoid letting location inhibit me from doing what's best for students. Also, I let the texts set the agenda. Keep in mind, I work to ensure my students' lives are represented in the texts I select so my students' lives and interests are setting the agenda for the work we do together.

Start slow but remember that discomfort is a prerequisite for growth. I had a conversation this week with a teacher who realized that her discomfort was preventing her from approaching "tough" topics with students, not her students' level of readiness.

These conversations are sustained through constant reflection, which means they must be considered during the planning process. However, these topics are standards to be mastered.

Q What are the most important things a teacher can do to make sure the future is a more empathic and justice-oriented one?

A First and foremost, model lives that are seeking justice and live empathetically with one another ourselves.

Q Are there good resources or people for me to follow to help me curate a more diverse classroom?

A The first question I ask myself: are my students' lives represented and how are they represented? I think it was Jessica Lifshitz who said, "If I follow the lead of my students I usually end up in a pretty good place." Second, I remember that this is work that I cannot do alone. Even the most well meaning of us have biases and blind spots that impact our ability to critically evaluate materials.

The Physical Environment

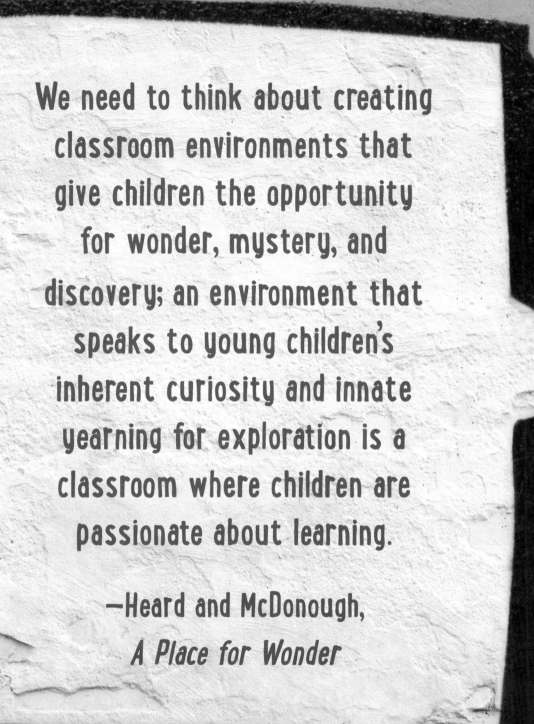

We need to think about creating classroom environments that give children the opportunity for wonder, mystery, and discovery; an environment that speaks to young children's inherent curiosity and innate yearning for exploration is a classroom where children are passionate about learning.

—Heard and McDonough,
A Place for Wonder

Introduction

Every decision we make as teachers is a reflection of our core beliefs and values. Just as the way we plan a math lesson or intentionally choose our read-alouds directly reflects what we value; so does the way we design the physical classroom environment. As teachers, we can take a look around our spaces and ask ourselves, "Does this space reflect what I value most about children and learning?"

Two big ideas drive our decisions as we set up and adapt our classroom environments:

The first big idea, *setting up your classroom: start with a blank canvas, not a finished masterpiece*, will guide you through the nut and bolts of preparing your classroom (from furniture arrangement to organizing materials).

The second big idea, *let your space reflect your students*, will help you create a fluid, evolving environment that reflects all of your students and empowers them as learners in your community.

No matter what the physical shell of your classroom might look like, you have the opportunity and potential to turn any space into an environment that reflects what you value. Not only does your classroom environment reflect what you and your class value as a community, but it also has the power to *shape* your community's values. Anita Olds wrote, "Our thoughts as reflected in our designs, in turn shape children's beliefs about themselves and life" (2000, 12–13). From the layout of the furniture to the feel of the room, from the materials you provide to the way your space evolves in response to your students, the environment itself can drive learning and community building.

Big Idea: Setting Up Your Classroom: Start with a Blank Canvas, Not a Finished Masterpiece

Think back to that sticky day in August when you first moved into your freshman dorm. You were no doubt loaded down with bags and boxes and that feeling of equal parts glee and terror. When you opened the door to your dorm room, chances are you were not wowed by the space that would be yours to share for the next nine months. Desks bolted down, lofted beds shoved into the only space they would fit, and a cable connection for the TV in the most awkward corner. That environment—completely predetermined for you—left very little sense of ownership, creativity, or belonging. Compare that with your first apartment or your first house. All of a sudden, you could think of dozens of ways to set up the furniture just to your liking, and you spent hours arranging the pictures on your living room wall. This space probably felt much more like a home—a place you felt comfortable, a place where you wanted to spend your time.

As classroom teachers, we have a choice of which kind of experience to offer our students. On their first days of school, they can walk into a dorm room version of their classroom—with all of the spaces set up just so, from the arrangement of the furniture to the borders of the bulletin boards. Or, alternatively, we can restrain ourselves from creating a perfectly curated room (save those Pinterest boards for home!) and have our students walk in, instead, to a blank canvas—a space ready to be transformed slowly, over time, by, with, and for the children in the class.

Although the biggest work of creating an environment that reflects your community will be done once your students arrive, there are still plenty of things to do in August and September to prime the canvas and prepare your room. When it comes to setting up a classroom environment, let "less is more" be your mantra. For our classrooms to reflect our beliefs about teaching, they must evolve over time. In August we create a blank slate, and by January we are teaching and learning in a space that is almost alive—alive with our class' unique personality, alive with the messy construction of knowledge and learning that we've done together, alive with the community we've built.

Room Aesthetic

Have you ever opened up a magazine or browsed online and seen a room that you want to leap right into? A cozy chair just begging for a reader, an immaculate kitchen ready for baking, a beautiful desk inspiring writing? There are certain elements that the environments where we do our best thinking, learning, collaborating, and creating have in common. They are well lit, beautiful, and carefully curated. The educators of Reggio Emilia, a small city in northern Italy, have spent decades thinking about how environments affect learning and community. The environments we create have the opportunity to be "a whole made up of different parts in harmony, balanced. Interaction of different elements (objects, situations, iconography, materials) that produces a tranquil result, a symphony of the individual parts" (Ceppi and Zini 1998, 26). When it comes to setting up our classrooms, there are certain choices that we can make as teachers to design an aesthetic that promotes independence, creativity, and joy. Compare the messages sent from a classroom that has desks in rows, facing a teacher's desk up front, versus a room with tables and no teacher's desk. The message of the first classroom suggests that all the children are there to acquire information from one person, the teacher, whereas the second suggests that the work of the classroom involves the collaborative engagement of all invited. Think critically about the message sent with each piece of furniture, and consider incorporating elements often eliminated from institutional environments. You don't have to have a huge budget or the newest IKEA design to create this kind of a classroom; with just a little bit of planning and some creativity, you can set up a beautiful, welcoming classroom space.

COLORS Although it's tempting and easy to outfit classrooms in primary colors, neutral and warm colors create a glow to a classroom. Natural woods and warm colors reflect light in a way that gives off a comforting, enveloping feeling (Zane 2015, 53). Think of your personal reaction to walking into a room splashed with reds, orange, and yellow (like Burger King) and you can see why calming, muted colors inspire a different kind of interaction between students.

SIMPLE, NOT OVERWHELMING Keep what you put on your walls to a minimum. Some teachers use a 80-20 or 90-10 rule—they want to have the students create (or be a part of creating) between 80 and 90 percent of what's on the walls of the room. Although this might make your room seem rather bare at first, there will be plenty to fill up your blank slate once your students arrive. It will also help your children thrive; a study by researchers from Carnegie Mellon University found that "children in highly decorated classrooms were more distracted, spent more time off-task and demonstrated smaller learning gains than when the decorations were removed" (Association of Psychological Science 2014). Though we are firm believers in visual supports for children, think critically about what children really need to be successful in the classroom.

GO MINIMALIST Get rid of anything that you don't think you'll use this year. If you're a first-year teacher coming into a classroom that has leftovers from the previous teacher, take the time to go through as much as you can. For every following year, consider going on a June cleaning spree and ask yourself, "Did I use this item this year?" if the answer is no, find a good home for it. Your room can reflect your own personal aesthetic, but just keep it in balance. Remember that once your students have settled in, if someone walks into your classroom, the room should reflect the authentic aesthetic of the children and should evolve and change over time. For more on things you can let go of and allowing your classroom to reflect your students, see the next section.

NATURAL LIGHT Think about how a walk outside can energize and ease your mind. Compare that to the buzz of florescent lights often heard in schools or offices. It's no surprise that some studies have found links between florescent lights and behavior issues. Use as much natural light in your room as you can. If possible, turn off the overhead florescent lights and light your room with a mix of natural light and small lamps. Situate spaces for children to gather and work near natural light and the pools of lamplight (Zane 2015, 48).

PLANTS Soften your room with easy-to-grow and easy-to-care-for plants such as aloe, philodendron, and spider plants. These plants do well in all light and add a natural element to school environments that can often feel a little sterile. Plants also offer a literal, visual representation of a growing, thriving community.

Room Arrangement

As teachers, we often spend the summer thinking and fantasizing about how our classroom will look. Then, we arrive, and somehow it is much smaller and there is much more furniture than we thought. Don't lose hope! The journey to a beautiful, functional classroom gets messy before it gets clean. Setting up our classroom furniture might seem haphazard at first—put a bookshelf here, a table there, writing supplies over there, but each decision we make has a significant impact on how our community interacts, functions, and thrives. The spaces we create affect where and how children gather and work, how twenty-plus bodies flow (or don't!) from one area of the room to another, and how children see themselves as agents of their own learning. Our goal should be to create a classroom where it's clear to children what they *can do* as opposed to needing to tell them what they cannot do. A cozy corner should say to them, "You can relax quietly here." A meeting area should say, "You can all come together as a community here." Each of these decisions intentionally build students' agency in their classroom and their learning.

When you're arranging your room, consider these guiding principles and questions

PERSPECTIVE What would the room look like from a child's-eye view? Think about this both literally and figuratively. If you teach young children, get down low and see the space at their eye level. Are there nooks and crannies and cozy spaces for them to hide and play? Are there spaces for older children to stand to work or sit comfortably in a meeting area?

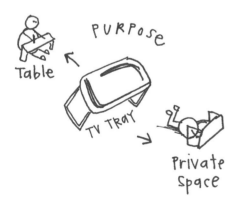

PURPOSE What is the purpose of each particular space? Is it a space for gathering as a whole class? A space for a few children to read? A space for building, making, and creating? Once you think about the purpose of each space, notice what other spaces are near it. Making small changes like moving your classroom library away from a noisier block area can have a lasting impact once all of the children arrive.

FLOW How will each space in your classroom be used over the course of the day? Go through the schedule of your day with an eye on your classroom's layout. Think about where children will be during each part of your day. If you take writing workshop as an example, visualize your class gathered for a minilesson, dispersing to various areas of the room to work, interacting in small groups, and then gathering again as a whole class. Try to proactively problem solve issues that you can imagine, such as busy transitions, access to community supplies, and the need for different environments for work.

KINDERGARTEN CLASSROOM MAP

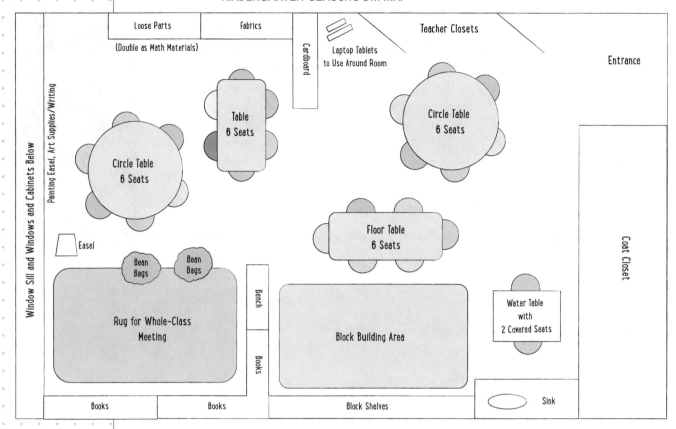

GRADES 1–2 CLASSROOM MAP

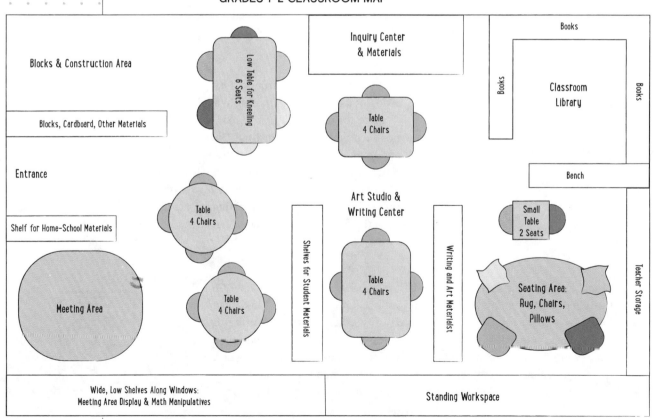

GRADES 3–5 CLASSROOM MAP

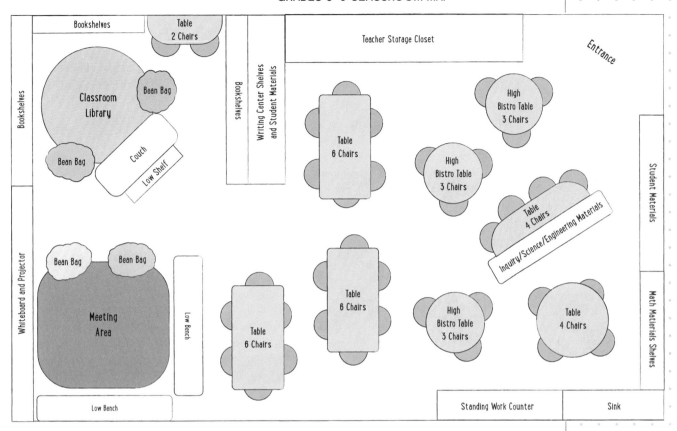

SKETCH YOUR OWN CLASSROOM MAP

Room Materials

Just as how we arrange our room reflects our view of children and learning, the materials we offer should do the same. As a rule of thumb, children should be able to access and use any material or supply that is at their level and visible to them. Tuck the scary paper cutter away and stash supplies in a closet or high up on shelves. If we want to build children's independence and agency, we should celebrate when they are accessing classroom materials to solve problems and aid their learning.

FLEXIBLE MATERIALS MEAN FLEXIBLE THINKERS Provide open-ended materials that students can access throughout the day. These flexible materials can range from writing supplies such as sharpies, markers, pens, pencils, and crayons to building and creating supplies such as tape, scissors, staples, cardboard, and fabric. Try to bring in materials with many possible uses: buttons, for example, can be used to sew up a cape for imaginary play, as counters in math, and as eyes on puppets to retell stories.

COMMUNITY SUPPLIES BUILD COMMUNITY Teach your students that they can access these community materials when they need to (Cut open those snack pouches! Staple your writing together! Build a carrier for your post it notes!), and, as a class community, set limits for their use (Take just a few sheets of blue paper at a time! Sharpies aren't for whiteboards! When a supply runs out, let someone know!). Sharing materials offers plenty of opportunities to build social skills and community experience and sets a tone of common vision and purpose.

INCLUSIVE MATERIALS Teacher and thinker extraordinaire Jess Lifshitz says, "The faces that greet our students from our bookshelves can be as powerful as the ones that greet them at the door" (@Jess5th, August 15, 2016). When you set up your classroom library, make sure your choices reflect a broad range of experiences, situations, and contexts. This should *not* look like a "multicultural" bin in the library, but rather all kinds of books where children can see themselves and their families. This extends to all the materials we bring into our classrooms. Does this item reflect all the children in the community? Family structures? Race? Jobs of parents and family members? Housing? Gender variations? The presence or absence of materials representing the children in your classroom sends a powerful message. "When children see themselves and their families reflected in their early childhood setting, they feel affirmed and that they belong. When children's identities and families are invisible, the opposite happens. Children feel that they are unimportant and do not belong" (Derman-Sparks and Edwards 2009, 13). For much more, see our interview with Chad Everett in Section 1 on page 29, and the resources he suggests.

SETTING UP SYSTEMS AND GETTING ORGANIZED One other important step to getting ready for the start of the year is to come up with systems to stay organized. It can seem daunting to say the least to organize your planning, your teaching materials, your files, and your students' materials. The good news is, you don't yet have to have all the answers. In fact, in may be beneficial to leave many of the student organization systems in the hands of your children. When Kristi first started teaching, she wanted color-coded folders for each subject that matched the color of the schedule card. She premade labels and bins and thought out every inch of organization. But sometimes the ebbs and flows of the classroom resisted the orderly boxes she wanted everything in. And sometimes the organizational plans she made did not make sense for the children she was forcing them on. Perhaps more importantly, she realized organizing *for* children takes away some of that independence and agency that is so critical for our classrooms. So what to do? Ask your children!

Present the problem as a challenge and brainstorm solutions: "Guys! Everyone keeps forgetting their take-home folders! What routine could we make to help ourselves?" This sends a critical message and some powerful teaching. The message is that when we are faced with a problem, we use our collective brainpower to solve it. The teaching is *how* to organize. Too often we skip the step of teaching thoughtful organization in favor of doing it ourselves, but what happens to those kiddos? They end up as middle schoolers who aren't sure how to pack their own backpacks or find anything in their lockers. Kristi waits until kids have multiple books they have written to ask, "Gosh, all this great stuff is getting out of hand! How can we keep our books safe and organized?" Christine has her students help organize, label, and manage the classroom library; when things get a bit chaotic, they have a class meeting *in* library. "Space books in the Ocean Animals bin? Uh-oh! How can we fix this place up?" If you worry about the time this takes, consider the time it takes for a child to dig a paper out of a messy backpack and then multiply that by every day of that human being's life. Sometimes a little time spent up front pays its dividends over decades.

For more on classroom environments check out:

Pedagogy and Space: Design Inspirations for Early Childhood Classrooms by Linda Zane (2015)

Designs for Living and Learning, Second Edition: Transforming Early Childhood Environments by Deb Curtis and Margie Carter (2014)

The Space: A Guide for Educators by Rebecca Louise Hare and Dr. Robert Dillon (2016)

Here are just a few ideas for putting systems for organization in place. We have given some options for student systems so that when you pose the question to your children, you have possibilities in mind if no one is sure how to organize, or a way to get started if you are not sure you want to hand over all the organization to children in the beginning.

ORGANIZATION CHALLENGE	OPTIONS FOR TEACHER
WORK IN PROGRESS	Try organizing your teaching materials by subject. Keep bins for each subject area and house copies and materials for upcoming teaching in each bin. Stash the materials you need for teaching as close as you can to where the teaching happens. Have a collection of more open-ended teaching materials such as markers, Post-it notes, paper, scissors, and so on next to where you teach minilessons or small groups to use on the fly.
BOOKS	Many teachers organize their books in a classroom library in a designated space in their classroom. There are many different ways to organize a classroom library. (For more on schoolwide and classroom organization of books, see It's *All About the Books* by Clare Landrigan and Tammy Mulligan [2018].) We suggest sorting books into bins based on topics and authors and series rather than strictly by level. Primary teachers might have a separate area to pull multiple copies of leveled texts for guided reading groups, but the books that are available for the children in the classroom should be organized the way they might be in a bookstore or a library. Then, you can teach your children to read the pictures of some and the words of others depending on their reading development.
COMPLETED WORK	Filing cabinets or binders can be organized by subject area or time of year. You might have a folder with plans and notes from the first week of school and another with materials for the first informational writing unit in your writing workshop. Google Drive and Google Docs are great tools for collaborating with other teachers and planning for instruction.
KEEPING TRACK OF GROWTH AND DATA	Apps like Notability and Evernote can help you take quick notes on a digital device while you meet with students and organize that information by student. Conferring clipboards for each subject area help your conferring work and student goals. Clipboards that also have a storage box are especially helpful, because they can double as your conferring toolkit. A binder or a set of folders organized by student can be used to store assessments that you want to keep for the year. For more on tracking your students' growth and responsive teaching, see Section 4, and for sample forms for conferring and data collection, see the appendixes.

Some children organize their work by folders, with a different folder for reading, writing, and so on. These folders can be collected and stored together or stored in individual students' cubbies.

Children can store their books in book baggies (either cloth bags made specifically for the purpose or large plastic bags work well) or book boxes. Some classrooms have clusters of six book boxes here and six book boxes there around the room to minimize traffic during transitions. Other classrooms have all the materials for one subject in one part of the room.

Set up binders to be portfolios of students' work. Save one item (such as one piece of writing from a unit) and send the rest home.

Digital tools like Seesaw (a student-friendly app and website) can be a nice complement to keeping hard copies of work. With Seesaw, you can easily snap a picture of students' work or take a video of their reading and save it in their digital portfolio.

Goal sheets in students' folders provide tangible reminders of what they are specifically working on and help them take ownership over their learning goals.

Big Idea: Let Your Space Reflect Your Students

So here they come. It's the first day of school and you're standing in your classroom—butterflies in your stomach, checking and rechecking your day's schedule, and making sure everything is set up just so. If you're anything like us, you're probably moving the table by the window an inch to the left and thanking a higher power that that recurring dream where your alarm doesn't go off didn't come true. There is nothing like the first day and the first few weeks of the school year. All of that work you've put in to set up your classroom is finally paying off—your students walk in and see before them a space ready to be transformed from a blank canvas to a living, breathing ecosystem. Over the course of the next nine months, your environment will be "taken up" by your class community. Small spaces will morph into cozy reading nooks, walls will reflect your co-constructed knowledge, a table near the window will be first a science lab, then a writing center, and then a story recording studio.

As a teacher, you're one of many cofacilitators of your classroom environment. Perhaps your best bet is to plan for the unplanned. So as your students enter on their very first day, even after you've poured so much blood, sweat, and tears into your space, let go of your expectations about what your classroom will look and feel like in ten minutes, in a month, or at the end of the year. Allow yourself and your students the flexibility to be spontaneous in how the classroom is arranged, what materials are presented, and what spaces are used for. In Reggio Emilia, educators call the environment the "third teacher" after the teacher and parents. Lella Gandini writes, "In order to act as an educator for the child, the environment has to be flexible: it must undergo frequent modification by the children and the teachers in order to remain up-to-date and responsive to their needs to be protagonists in constructing their knowledge" (1998, 177). The more voice and control students are given in co-constructing their classroom environment, the more they will see themselves as valued members of the community, with strong senses of belonging, agency, and independence.

What needs to get done before day one? (And trust us, it will probably get changed on day two.)

- ♥ Clear it out.
- ♥ Bring in plants.
- ♥ Think about lighting.
- ♥ Set up the furniture.
- ♥ Organize and put out essential materials for the first week.
- ♥ Set up the classroom library but leave room for changes in bins and labels.
- ♥ Find flexible seating options.
- ♥ Minimize your own space.
- ♥ Put only a few things up on the walls.
- ♥ Prepare basic organizational systems for yourself and students.

IDEAS FOR THE FIRST FEW DAYS OF SCHOOL

Here are a few other things you might plan to do with your students in the first few days of school that will help set the tone that this is **their** classroom, not just **your** classroom:

LABELS → Instead of rushing to do this before the children arrive, have students label different materials, areas of the classroom, library book bins, folders, and notebooks. Primary-grade classes can kill two birds with one stone and do this as a series of interactive writing lessons.

SELF-PORTRAITS → Invite students to paint or draw pictures of themselves and hang these on the walls.

PHOTOGRAPHS → Snap pictures of your students on the first day and put these on labels and then add to cubbies, the word wall, or book boxes. You could also use these photographs in routine charts such as "What to Do First Thing" or "Reading Workshop Routines."

BOOK DISPLAY → Survey students about their reading interests, favorite authors and series, and work together to display these in your classroom library.

On Your Mark, Get Set, Change It Up!

If you're trying to create the most flexible environment possible, this might mean that you need to make changes right away. Take time to watch how your students are using the space and where and when they gravitate toward specific spaces. If something doesn't seem to be working for your class, ask for your students' feedback and problem solve the issue as a community. On the first day of school in Christine's first grade, several members of her class were trying to build with blocks and play school on a whiteboard easel in the same space. After choice time, the class sat down and Christine asked, "It seemed a little cramped in this corner of the classroom today. What could we move around so that the block crew can build and the school kids can play, too?" Together, the class brainstormed moving the easel over to another corner of the classroom. Christine could have easily made this switch midplay or even at lunch, but by involving the students she set the tone that they had control over their classroom environment, that they could problem solve when trouble came up, and that their voices, ideas, and needs were valued in this space. In Kristi's kindergarten class, large bulky tables were replaced by light, collapsible ones after she noticed how her students wanted to move the tables around based on what they were working on.

As Elsa Says, "Let It Go"

To truly create and sustain a dynamic physical classroom environment, you'll have to consider giving up some practices that *seem* to be very necessary to every classroom experience. These practices include some of the very images traditionally associated with what

	WHY IT MAY SEEM APPEALING
TEACHER-CURATED ART, MATH, WRITING MATERIALS	Keeping materials in the closet and pulling out just what your students need for a specific lesson can seem really appealing—everything stays organized and nothing gets misplaced or overused.
PREMADE, LAMINATED CHARTS	We get it—you spend hours making a stunning chart showing just how your reading workshop will go. Why not send it through the industrial strength laminator and save it to use year after year?
BEAN TABLE AND GUIDED READING TABLE	In many classrooms, a bean table or a guided reading table doubles as a teacher's desk. The teacher sits on one side and the students sit on another; at first glance, this seems like the perfect arrangement for teaching small groups.
TEACHER DESK	There is nothing more central to the iconic classroom vision than the teacher's desk. Years ago it was front and center—the wheel from which the captain charted the class' course. More recently, teachers' desks have been tucked off to the side of the classroom and used as a space to get work done and store Important Teacher Things.

it means to be a "good" teacher: perfectly manicured bulletin boards, a teacher's desk complete with apple, children sitting in their assigned seats—but let's take a closer look at some of these practices.

WHAT YOU MIGHT TRY INSTEAD

Having designated classroom supplies helps your students take responsibility for those supplies and sends the message that the tools are there for their learning. Additionally, students can learn to use different materials flexibly and to solve problems. Soon you'll see your kindergarteners using scissors to open their own snacks—something they wouldn't be able to do if the scissors were up and out of reach on a shelf.

As the adage goes, you can't teach responsibility without giving children responsibility; let classroom supplies be your first step.

The impact of using charts with children actually comes from constructing the charts *with* the children; the more involved they are, the better. Charts should be tools for learning and thinking, not beautiful displays of art. When you're done using a chart with your students, snap a quick picture of it to remind yourself for next year and then say your good-byes.

The downside of a bean table is that its design lends itself only to *one type* of arrangement. If our goal is to have flexible classrooms, then our tables must have flexible purposes. Small groups are just as easily run on the rug or at any table in your classroom. In fact, other tables actually lend themselves to guided reading. It's much easier to pop up and down coaching each child without having to clamber out from behind the bean.

Here's the thing about teachers' desks: chances are, if you're doing your job, you are rarely at your desk. Chances are, also, if you're anything like us, your desk becomes a repository for stacks and stacks of papers, sticky notes, and miscellaneous items. Instead of taking up room in the classroom (and sending the message that this desk is *not* a place for children), you might consider storing your papers and Important Teacher Things in a closet or on a shelf and picking a big table in the classroom to do your work when you need too. You'll find that a big space in your classroom is freed up and can be repurposed for a useful and accessible spot for children.

(continues)

THEMED BULLETIN BOARDS	Many, many teachers we know take such pride in how their bulletin boards represent their creativity, their class' work, and the pride they take in their students. And, if you have perfectionist tendencies like many of us, creating lovely displays can feel quite rewarding. Teacher-curated bulletin boards can showcase the best versions of what's happening in our classrooms and what our students create.
CUTE FONTS	Google "teacher fonts" and you'll get hundreds of images of curlycues and bubble letters and things that scream (to our adult eyes) *kids!* To us, many of these fonts seem to be the perfect way to make what we're doing more accessible and engaging to our students.

When we hold these long-standing practices up to our core beliefs about learning, many things that we've been taught (and have even taught others!) are "must-dos" for classrooms to function well are actually infringing on our ability to build an ecosystem for growth, agency, and belonging.

If Your Walls Could Talk, They'd Tell the Story of Your Community

One of the things we love most about teaching is that no class is exactly like any class that came before it or any class that will follow. Even if you teach the same grade in the same school for decades, there will never be two years that are exactly the same. The needs and interests of individual students, combined with the unique culture that a group of children creates, means that every year offers opportunities for spontaneity and new opportunities. And these interests and needs can and should be reflected in your classroom's physical environment. If we start every year with a blank canvas classroom, it can be tempting to let our spaces reflect the routines of the season. September? Better get down the box on apples and falling leaves. May? Time for spring flowers. But something much more powerful can happen if we listen to and are led by the interests and needs of our students. One year, Christine's third-grade class got so interested in writing and acting out fairy tales that they transformed the classroom library into a puppet theater. Another year, fascinated by the number 1,000, her students set a goal to make and hang 1,000 paper snowflakes before spring. In Kristi's classroom, a gigantic snowstorm and its aftermath meant buckets of snow brought in for

Don't get us wrong, we're big fans of puns and beautiful, artistic displays. But we believe that bulletin boards should be a place to document and celebrate your students' work. Bulletin boards don't need to be perfect; they should be authentic representations of the writing, math, reading, or inquiry work your class engages in. Just as your students have a say in how things look in the classroom, let your students have a say in how their learning will be displayed to the larger community, too.

In reality, many of those fancy fonts don't match the way we teach our students to form letters. It's best if the fonts we use are clear and easy to read and that every letter is easily identifiable. Imagine being a first grader trying to read a label with an *A* that has polka dots and squiggles. Suddenly the reading become much more difficult. Fonts can be fun, serious, playful, spooky, loud, or quiet—just make sure you're picking your fonts mindfully and for a purpose, not just to be cute and kiddy.

study, measurements on the wall of how high it reached, and snow-centric read-alouds dominating the tabletops.

We'll discuss negotiating a responsive curriculum much more in Section 4, but the transformations that happen to your physical classroom can be influenced by many things:

⭐ **The interests of your students:** maybe a strong interest in Star Wars, space, or basketball means that you pull out more books on that topic or that you rearrange the classroom to facilitate Star Wars play or a homemade planetarium or a giant March Madness bracket.

⭐ **The community around you:** Perhaps your students are especially engaged in elections and want a space to gather information and respond. Or maybe there's been a major weather event in your area and your students are interested in setting up a way to help. Local construction could launch an inquiry unit or a whole different setup for block building.

⭐ **The curriculum that you introduce:** Just as we want our students to drive our curriculum, we want our curriculum to drive our spaces. If you're studying geology, then you could have a space in your classroom for soil samples or rocks or, if you're really lucky or industrious, a stream table. If you're writing narratives, then create a space where children can take the "stage" and act out their stories—even if it's just a temporary curtain or a square of masking tape on the rug.

In addition to creating spaces that reflect your whole-class community, there are some very subtle but important ways that your physical space can meet the needs of your students, as well.

Flexible Seating and Work Spaces: It's About Learning, Not Sitting Still

As teachers, we're told over and over again that our students thrive on predictability, routine, and structure. At first glance, assigned seats might seem to create a sense of that order. Children know exactly where they're supposed to go when you send them off from the rug and where to go when you ask them to "take their seats." When Christine and Kristi start talking about *not* having assigned seats for students (and, yes, we're talking all ages here!), a ripple of shock and questioning always goes around the room. But if you think carefully about *why* you want your students to have assigned seats, chances are the reasons are rooted in your desire for order, not for what is best for children. Instead of teaching "go to your spot and get to work" we teach, "find a good spot for you and get to work."

If you're anything like us, you have a different spot for writing or planning than you do for reading. Just as we've taken time to set up a variety of spaces around the room—cozy nooks and big meeting areas—we should take the time to help our students find the spaces that best meet their needs depending on what they're doing. But rest assured, flexible seating doesn't mean that students just run all over the classroom for the entirety of a writing or reading workshop. Instead, you can guide your students to find the places that work best for them to write or read or play or do math. Often our students fall into natural routines or rhythms of being in certain places that work well for them and return to them day after day.

Let's follow one of Christine's second-grade students over the course of the day and see what flexible seating might look like to a seven-year-old.

MORNING MEETING	Jacob is sitting on a low bench in the circle where he can wiggle without bumping anyone else.
CHOICE TIME	Jacob is in the block corner constructing the trash compactor scene from Star Wars—he's up, down, low, high, a blur of movement.
READING	Jacob is under a table with a pillow and then kneeling on a pillow at a small group at a low table with Christine.
WRITING	Jacob is standing by the window at a higher table where he can rock back and forth a bit. Later, he grabs a clipboard and sits under the table.
READ-ALOUD	Jacob is again sitting on the low bench at the meeting area.
MATH	Jacob is sitting at a table with his math partner and then goes to the rug for a small group with Christine. He lies down on his stomach and props his head in his hands.
INQUIRY	Jacob is working with a group of four at a larger table. He alternates between standing and sitting.
INTERACTIVE WRITING/CLOSING CIRCLE	Jacob is standing at the back of the group—shifting a bit in his own space, but engaging with the whole-class closing activity.

The key to flexible seating and spaces is to create a classroom environment that offers enough spaces and flexibility for children to learn in the way that best helps their bodies and brains. But, as with any new thing, there may be a few bumps as you give this a try in your classroom. Here are a few tips for making flexible seating work well in your classroom:

⭐ Before you introduce flexible seating, think about just how flexible you want to be. Are you OK with having children work under tables? On tables? If not, why not? We all have our limits and reasons; just make sure yours are clear because your students will ask.

⭐ Introduce every type of seating and every space for working to your students strategically and allow them to all try each space out.

⭐ Have students reflect on where they work best and why.

⭐ Create guidelines with your class for certain spaces at certain times of the day—perhaps there's a table by the window for children who need a quieter space to work and another space across the room for children who like to chat more as they write.

⭐ Solve problems as they arise (and there will be problems). You might be tempted to revert back to the good old days of assigned seats when a specific table of mathematicians isn't superfocused. Instead, take a problem-solving approach and include the students.

⭐ Remember to keep your focus on engagement, not just compliance. If a child moves from a standing spot to the rug but keeps writing, that seems to reflect what he needed as a learner in that moment. However, if a child moves six times in fifteen minutes and doesn't read any of her book, there's a problem to solve together.

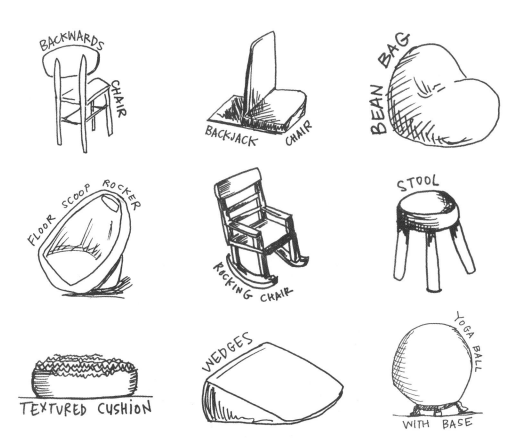

BACKWARDS CHAIR

BACKJACK CHAIR

BEAN BAG

FLOOR SCOOP ROCKER

ROCKING CHAIR

STOOL

TEXTURED CUSHION

WEDGES

YOGA BALL WITH BASE

Visuals and Schedules Support *All* Students

Another powerful way that you can meet the needs of students in your classroom is to use visual supports and schedules. Some of these supports—such as charts that teach routines, a daily schedule with pictures, and labels, to name a few—are designed to be accessed by the whole class. Other supports are specifically designed to meet the needs of individual students.

Too often the bulk of our teaching is oral. Imagine sitting through one of your grad school courses without being able to take notes, receive handouts, or have access to the lecture at another time. All but a few of us would have lost most of the information before the class ended. Rather than put our students in this situation, we make visual reminders of our teaching, called *charts*. The best charts:

For much more on charts and visual supports, read Kristi's *Smarter Charts* books, coauthored with Marjorie Martinelli (2012, 2014).

* ⭐ are made with students
* ⭐ reflect current teaching and thinking
* ⭐ include visuals and spare language
* ⭐ reduce the load on student memory.

Conclusion: Take Time to Reflect on Your Classroom and Your Beliefs

As the year moves along, it's easy for us to become caught up in and consumed by how we're teaching reading, writing, and math. You might look around your room and notice charts from September still lingering in December or a table for science inquiry that hasn't been touched (by you or your students) for weeks. Take this opportunity to take stock of your classroom environment and make adjustments as needed. Here are some guiding questions to help you with this process:

★ Does this classroom show how we value children as innovators, contributors, and agents of their learning? Does this environment promote student belonging, agency, and independence?

★ Does this space support flexibility and innovation?

★ Does this environment reflect our responsiveness as teachers? Does this space evolve and change over time?

★ How can the space better provoke and facilitate learning based on the interests and needs of the students?

★ How does the environment demonstrate that every member of our community is valued and respected?

Our physical classroom environments can communicate our beliefs about children and learning and school and community just as clearly as how we interact with children. The more our rooms are shaped for and by our students, the more likely they are to support our students' growth and development. The spaces themselves not only support our students' academic learning, but also nurture social and emotional skills such as self-regulation, problem solving, and responsibility—the very heart of our class community.

INTERVIEW

Julie Denberg is an occupational therapist in a school setting in New York. We asked her to help us understand what classroom teachers need to know about occupational therapy (OT) and how can they collaborate with providers.

Q What is OT? What does an occupational therapist do?

A OT helps people of all ages participate and function maximally in their everyday life. Many people hear *occupation* and they think OTs help people get jobs. In an OT's eyes, your jobs are your everyday activities. We help people to gain (or regain) skills, modify tasks, adapt the environment, provide supports, and educate or teach new skills to clients and their families and teachers in order to perform their daily activities (aka, occupations) to their highest potential.

Q Why might children see an occupational therapist?

A A child's occupation includes play, self-care, learning, and social interactions. Basic play skills assist children in gaining the necessary components for success in school, at home, and within their communities, which is why OT often looks like play.

Children receive OT to increase their independence in these skill areas. While "playing," occupational therapists are working on fine motor skills (pinch, grasp, strengthening), gross motor skills (whole body movement, muscle strength, endurance), graphomotor skills (handwriting), visual perceptual skills (processing and understanding visual information from the environment), visual motor skills (eye-hand coordination), activities of daily living (self-help skills such as dressing and feeding), sensory processing and integration (including adapting the environment), and often socialization skills.

In schools, occupational therapists work on all of these skills to create the best environment and increase function and independence for our students. It's about finding what foundational components are impeding our kids from being able to write, attend to a task, or engage with peers—function at their highest capacity. This can include working on core and body strength and endurance, which in turn can increase attention and fine motor skills. It can be teaching a student to recognize when they are not attending and what to do in that moment, or when they are fidgeting with everything in the room and how they rather can use those fidgets to help them focus. It can include teaching the steps of unpacking, or tying shoes. Occupational therapists help children in school to engage using visual and tactile cues, timers, and environmental adaptations to increase not only independence and function, but also self-esteem.

"Occupational therapists help children to engage using visual and tactile cues, timers, and environmental adaptations."

Q What are some common misconceptions about children who see occupational therapists?

A I wish I could help everybody! Unfortunately, OT services don't always "cure" what children are struggling with. It is important to note that tools and supports that occupational therapists provide can help *all* students, but because a strategy is helpful does not mean your child needs to receive services.

My hope is that teachers and families begin to use a universal design model [A universal design for learning model (UDL) is an educational framework where teachers design curriculum, materials, and the environment flexibly to allow for inclusion, differentiation, and access.] so that supports are available to all kids, whether they have an IEP [individualized education plan] or not. For example, a student who is demonstrating difficulty sustaining attention can benefit from the use of a butterfly 8 card, body breaks in between (or during) work, a seat cushion, or the option to stand. But this student does not necessarily require services. We just need to provide strategies to support him in being independent and successful.

In addition, a commonly misused term is that a student is *sensory*. [This is often (mis)used as a catch-all term to describe a student who gets overwhelmed by sights, sounds, touches, and textures.] Guess what, we're all sensory! We live in a sensory-rich world. It's how we cope in different sensory situations that can describe whether or not we truly have difficulty with sensory processing. When a student doesn't like the smell of things, or prefers to be in darker places, this is not enough information to say that your student has a sensory processing disorder.

Q What does it mean if a child has sensory issues?

A Good question! Sensory integration really is an abstract and difficult concept to understand. So let's try to look at it from a much simpler standpoint and think about how it affects our kids in school. When we look at it this way, we can better pinpoint what it is that our kids need and the tools that we can use to best support them.

Just like we break down words in reading, let's do it with *sensory*. "Senses" stands out most, right? So, we're looking at senses in the school environment, and how this environment affects our kids' senses. Our students are constantly impacted by what they see and smell, what they taste and hear, and what they touch. There are two more "hidden" senses that most people don't think or even know about. They're called *proprioception* and *vestibular input*.

The *proprioceptive system* tells the brain where the body is in space in relation to other objects, and then how to move. Children who lack eye-hand coordination and/or have difficulties with controlling their body are those who are often demonstrating problems regulating their proprioceptive system. This is why we, occupational therapists, apply deep pressure to some students. It helps their brains better understand where their arms and hands are in relation to the rest of their body.

The *vestibular system* also tells the brain where the body is in space, but relating to movement and head position. This can be seen with kids who rock, or can demonstrate calm and focus with use of a rocking chair, rather than a desk chair.

So what does this all mean? Children with sensory issues demonstrate difficulty reacting with appropriate automatic responses. For example, when we go outside on a sunny day, we often put on our sunglasses, use our hands to block the sun, or even squint our eyes. These are typical and automatic (we don't think about it) responses. A child with a sensory processing difficulty is unable to make that adaptive response. This child may yell, rock, grab on tightly to you, run in circles, demonstrate inability to self-calm, among other things. These are the children with true sensory difficulties.

I worked with a student who used to cry and scream at the top of his lungs at random moments throughout the day. It made the teachers and students around him *crazy*. What was this about? We knew this student was sensitive to touch and sound, but the slightest things were setting him off from 0 to 10 in a matter of seconds. He didn't want noise-canceling headphones, or a compression vest, or an adaptive chair, or a quiet space. However, when this friend came to the OT room, a low-lit room often with calming music, you could see his whole body immediately calm. Once he was calm, he was able to say "I'm hungry." A crunchy, salty pretzel snack completely turned him around. It was that easy! Often, we need to get down to our students' level and work with them to figure out what changes we can make to allow them to better function in our often overstimulating school environment. It can be simple environmental adaptations that allow them to feel more present in our world.

Q What are some things I can do to make every child feel more comfortable in my classroom?

A I feel that it is our responsibility, as teachers and therapists, to provide opportunities for all students to thrive in our environments while experiencing these sensitivities and learning how to process these sensations.

Think about the previous example of stepping out into the sunny day. How does that student feel when he steps into the iridescent lights in your classroom? Does he need sunglasses? Can we dim the lights or find opportunities to work with adaptive lighting (lamps, lanterns) throughout the room instead? Start by taking a step back and looking at your classroom as a whole. Are the bright, iridescent lights always on? Are there places students can sit other than in a chair, and is there a place they can stand to do their work as well? Try to think of ways that you can incorporate different opportunities for our friends to feel regulated (calm and in control) in a sensory-rich environment.

"I feel that it is our responsibility, as teachers and therapists, to provide opportunities for all students to thrive in our environments while experiencing these sensitivities and learning how to process these sensations."

The Emotional Environment

Human nature exists
and operates in an
environment. And it is
not "in" that environment
as coins are in a box,
but as a plant is in the
sunlight and soil.

—John Dewey,
"Morals Are Human"

Introduction

Creating a beautiful and inviting classroom is not just a physical act, it's an emotional one as well. It is also one that can be fraught with challenge and uncertainty. Our teaching degree, wishes, and hopes alone do not always prepare us to protect the emotional lives of a whole classroom of small beings. Sometimes we react to behaviors on instinct, sometimes we do what was done to us as students or children, sometimes we look at the quiet line of the neighbor down the hall and adopt her technique without question. The good news is that there is lots of research in the world to teach us how to be better caretakers of the emotional and social well-being of our charges. Some of it has to do with how we handle our expectations, some with how we handle our own reactions, some with how we respond to children and the way we teach them how to be in a community. Ultimately, our classrooms are microcosms of the world, and we want them to be places where we, too, would want to live. This section aims to guide you through some core principles of building emotionally stable, productive, and safe classrooms.

There are some big ideas that we have adopted, and these, like our core beliefs, are the skeletal elements on which our classroom communities are built.

The first big idea, *scheduling for success*, is based on the concept that we can build emotionally sound classrooms and prevent misbehaviors when we schedule our days with the developmental needs of children in mind. We will look at what research says about willpower and movement and study a few schedules for what makes them work for teachers and kids alike.

The next big idea, *build a community, don't just manage one*, makes the case that being a productive community member is something we learn through instruction, not punishment, and certainly not by just being managed. We will study how teachers set a tone for a positive, joyful classroom without relying on traditional management strategies like clip charts and stickers.

This brings us to one of the most important ideas of all, *social skills can be taught*, which lays out protocols for teaching any social skill. We will look at some real classrooms along the way to see the variety of ways we can teach the art of being a better human.

And of course, our final idea, *supporting every child*, is built on the premise that there is something that can help every child. Sometimes it is how we react, sometimes it is what we say, and sometimes it is what we do, but every child has a place in a happy, productive classroom.

We didn't know any of these ideas when we first started teaching (sorry, first five to seven years of kids!). We made lots of choices we now regret when it came to building emotional environments, emphasizing control over community and compliance over critical thinking. It's only through studying our classrooms, current research, and our own tendencies that we have made change. And we are still learning to make better choices day by day. This section, like the ones before it, is meant to be a little bit of a life raft in a big sea of ideas. So jump aboard; we can make a better world when we make better classroom communities.

Big Idea: Scheduling for Success

> How we spend our days is, of course, how we spend our lives.
> What we do with this hour, and that one, is what we are doing.
>
> —Annie Dillard, *The Writing Life*

If our classroom environments can play such a huge role in the creation of bustling, energized, independent communities, what else might be under our control that can have a similarly powerful effect? We make myriad choices to support the type of community we hope to build, not the least of which is how we plan to spend our days. In the biz, we call this a "daily schedule." How, when, and what we schedule can have a huge impact on the emotional life of our classrooms. A daily schedule built with child development in mind can prevent a whole host of issues and can help produce a whole lot of magic.

Scheduling in a Perfect World Versus Scheduling in the Real World

Let's all take a moment and go to a teaching fantasyland. This is a magical place where there are no rules, no standards, no bells, no periods, and no requirements beyond what children need. Ahh, breathe deep of this freedom, because we are all just visiting—though we can take some important ideas with us. How would children plan their day if they were allowed to dictate the whole thing? And not just imaginary, metaphorical children, but Alec and Diamond and Tomas and Sophie? When would they go outside? When would they pick up books? How would they use writing? What ways would they use the math materials? What questions would they ask, and how would schools work to serve our children's passions, rather than children serving schools' agendas? There are schools, and children lucky enough to be in them, where teachers build curriculum and schedules based on the interests and the passions of the children within them. Many of us feel as far away from this as possible when our district hands us a schedule to be followed to the minute in the week before we start school. Though we cannot transform all schools overnight into places designed by children, we can certainly push the balance of choice and power in the direction of our students in any school. What important ideas can we carry forward?

The Role of Willpower: Balancing Structured and Unstructured Activities

Researchers Roy Baumeister, Kathleen Vohs, and Dianne Tice (2007) found that using willpower to resist temptation (in one study, freshly baked cookies) made people more likely to give up on the next task (a difficult puzzle). Study after study has found that using self-control is an exhausting experience. "Every day, in one form or another, you exert willpower. You resist the urge to surf the Web instead of finishing your expense report. You reach for a salad when you're craving a burger. You bite your tongue when you'd like to make a snide remark. Yet a growing body of research shows that resisting repeated temptations takes a mental toll. Some experts liken willpower to a muscle that can get fatigued from overuse" (American Psychological Association). This is known in the field of psychology as "willpower depletion." The thing about willpower depletion is that there is not a whole lot you can do when you are all out of self-control. If you've been working on errands all day and have guests coming over, even if you want the bathroom to be clean, you may have to sit on the couch for fifteen minutes before you are physically able to get up and do it. The same holds true for kids. They may want to do what you ask, but they need a few moments to reboot and recenter before that is even a possibility.

Willpower depletion in school looks a lot like off-task behavior. Giving up, avoiding work, distracting others, or taking a loooooong trip to the bathroom might be a child's way of telling you they are all tapped out. Look at your daily schedule. Consider how much willpower you are asking a child to exert on any given day. Is it unrelenting? And consider it from a child's point of view. Recess could be the trickiest time of the day for a child if the rules are counter to that child's way of moving and playing. An expectation that kids come in "fresh" from recess assumes that they didn't spend thirty minutes being told "no" repeatedly. When our schedules set kids up to follow someone else's rules and desires *without a break*, we create and sustain their misbehaviors.

One way that we can address willpower depletion is by taking a close look at the amount of time we are asking children to be in structured or unstructured activities.

STRUCTURED ACTIVITIES	UNSTRUCTURED ACTIVITIES
Anything that requires a child to subvert his or her will to do a series of steps or tasks outlined by someone else	Anything where the choice/project/ partners/possibilities are in the hands of the child

A fire drill is a structured activity, following the rules in Simon Says is a structured activity, and most of our traditional academic teaching is a structured activity. The problem with only having structured activities is that children are not allowed to develop skills like organization, responsibility, problem solving, or creativity; plus, these activities exhaust a child in the same way they would exhaust us.

TIP!

Code your schedule with

HS (highly structured),

S (structured),

MS (minimally structured),

and see—do you have a run of all highly structured? Can you introduce a break earlier on? Could you join with another teacher so one could take kids outside and another could stay in with kids who just want to draw? Try a work choice, being mindful not to impose too many rules (thus making it highly structured) and see how that impacts your day.

Many teachers fear that chaos will reign supreme if the boundaries are lifted, but that may only be the case if the boundaries are rarely lifted. When we build a balanced diet of teacher choice and kid choice activities into every day, everyone benefits. Children learn the best ways of tackling projects, using materials, and working with others; they have opportunities to practice responsibility and organization; and they learn to follow through over time. Like anything, the more access children have to unstructured time, the better they are at managing it.

So what does a reasonable blend of structured and unstructured time look like? It could be that after your reading workshop (moderately structured) you have some time for kids to make a "work choice" (minimal structure), meaning they could keep reading books, but they could go work on writing or pick up on an art project they want to finish. Some kids may choose to play a math game or work on a book of fashion designs. You would likely generate possibilities as a community, eliminating things like playing tag, with clear reasons like the classroom is too small for that. You might think about the most highly structured part of your day and follow it with "free choice," opening it up for kids to dance to GoNoodle, lay on bean bags and gossip, or go for a quick run in the hallway to burn out some energy. Though this may feel like time away from work, it actually makes all work more meaningful and impactful. Think about how refreshed you are after a ten-minute break. That is how the human brain works; you can't be on someone's agenda for six hours straight without going a little batty.

Give More Choices

This is perhaps the easiest and most overlooked way to combat willpower depletion and shift the locus of power from teacher to child. Also, if there has been a heartbeat or thread in this book up to these pages, it is that we have to invert and subvert the old power structure of schools. Having children pass through minidictatorships year after year does not build a society of active problem solvers and advocates for justice and equality. We are not saying that you do nothing and let *Lord of the Flies* unfold in front of you, rather that we think it's important to teach and model how to share power, handle responsibility, and make sure each voice in the world is represented and heard. That may seem like a lofty goal to tie in with making a schedule, but when we let children make choices and have power, we set them up to be more successful in life. If you are not deeply tied to a district or school schedule, you can let children design the daily schedule for the community. Perhaps children set their own learning plans for the day by making a list of the jobs they want to accomplish, or maybe the community has a discussion and sets up the day based on what the group feels. Not all of us have this flexibility, but we do have choices.

If you have a less flexible schedule—maybe the times and even the lessons are set out for you—be creative in finding the flexibility we discussed in the first section. Even if someone will come in to check to see that you're doing "writing workshop" at 9:45 every day, there are still many ways to offer your students choices. What children write, the materials they use, the shape of their books, and the space they work in can all be put into their hands. For every choice you have to make for a child (now is writing time), what two choices can you give back?

Does it matter if they write in pen or pencil? On white paper or pink? About a real event or an event they wish were real? We assure you that children can meet Common Core writing benchmarks at any level writing with a pink gel pen on unlined paper while sitting in a bean bag about a topic of their own personal choosing. In fact, we argue they are more likely to meet benchmarks in that way because instead of fighting meaningless will-power battles (stay in the chair, don't get up to sharpen that dull pencil, stay on the lines), they are free to focus on the actual thinking work of writing.

Now extend this to reading, writing, math, and whatever else is in your day. Maybe there are three math groups you want to meet with, but when students are not with you, they can make a plan to play a math game, complete an investigation, or work on their own math questions in the order they think will work best for them. Or perhaps if you do literacy centers, children can choose the order they go in each center. This will not go smoothly at first. Why would it? This does not mean you abandon ship. Take the information you get from the first day to help you teach how to make better choices the next day. And so on and so on.

When we give children choice, we also teach them how to make choices wisely and prepare them for a life of decision making. Even small choices carry big messages: I trust you, you are capable, you are in charge here. When we give choice, we also eliminate the self-control landmines that can deplete willpower, and a formerly narrow task becomes wide enough for each child to find joy and pleasure within it.

Look at your schedule and ask: Where do children have choice in the day? Where can I increase it? Eliminating a morning do now in favor of an open choice of activities might be enough to change the tone of a day and show you other windows of choice to expand.

These two back-to-back activities mean that the first thirty minutes may place the highest demands on willpower. Children may come from environments before school that were also placing demands on their willpower, meaning that they are not likely to have a high-success start because they are already working with depletion.

More on these structures in later sections.

For more on choice time, see Renée Dinnerstein's book: *Choice Time.*

For more on inquiry in the primary classroom, see Smokey Daniels' *The Curious Classroom.*

First-Grade Schedule (Before)	
Schedule Item	Level of Structure
Morning math "do now" and unpack	Highly structured
Morning meeting with shared reading/interactive writing	Highly structured
Writing workshop	Moderately structured/ some choice
Morning outside recess break	Moderately structured/ some choice
Reading workshop	Moderately structured/ some choice
Read-aloud	Highly structured
Lunch and recess (seats assigned)	Highly structured
Math	Moderately structured/ some choice
Choice time	Unstructured
Inquiry (social studies/ science)	Moderately structured/ some choice
Specialty class: gym/art/ music, etc.	Highly structured

Children have some choice here, which means that this time will allow for some willpower to reboot. For individual children who might love these times of day, reading and writing workshop and an outdoor break might make a full reboot. For children who struggle with some of these times, these components of the schedule may be more taxing than we anticipate, even with choice built in.

A highly structured activity right before one of the most challenging parts of the day for some children is a recipe for trouble. If you cannot adjust the rules around lunch (make seats free choice for example), carefully consider how you make sure children enter that time with the deepest reserves of self-control.

This afternoon seems to allow children opportunities to explore and create on their own terms, as long as they have not had them "taken away" by behaviors we may have created by a high-stress morning schedule.

First-Grade Schedule (After)	
Schedule Item	**Level of Structure**
Morning work choice	Unstructured
Morning meeting with shared reading/interactive writing	Highly structured
Writing workshop	Moderately structured/ some choice
Morning break—free choice, partner with another teacher for indoor/outdoor play options	Unstructured
Read-aloud	Highly structured
Reading workshop	Moderately structured/ some choice
Lunch and recess	Moderately structured/ some choice
Free work choice	Unstructured
Math	Moderately structured/ some choice
Choice time	Unstructured
Inquiry (social studies/science)	Moderately structured/ some choice
Specialty class: gym/art/music, etc.	Highly structured

This open-ended time allows children to enter, recenter, and prepare for the day ahead.

Building in just one more choice—stay in or go out—allows children to make choices more in line with what they might desire to do. Not everyone finds the playground a break; some children just want quiet time to write and draw.

If seats are unassigned and rules are relaxed a little, this time can become easier for children.

Moving this away from lunch allows children to focus fully on the job at hand yet still have time to regain energy before lunch.

This addition allows children to take a mental break after recess while still being productive.

Focus on Process

There is no surer way to cause a breakdown in a smooth running classroom than to insist that everyone produce the same end product. When did this become a worthwhile goal of education? Since when have innovation and progress been achieved by everyone following the exact same steps to the exact same outcome? We think this confusion has to do with a misconception that learning produces a product, as opposed to the development of a process. When we focus on the process we want children to develop, we can let go of the sameness of product idea to demonstrate mastery.

When Kristi started working at the Teachers College Reading and Writing Project, one of the first think tanks she participated in was an adult book club. She thought it was odd until the group met to talk about the book. Where Kristi had just read for plot and questions, the rest of the group had read with an eye on their process. She listened as her colleagues discussed their reading process and broke down each task step by step. Where Kristi had written Post-its that said, "Knew this guy would be trouble," others in the group had gone a step further to ask themselves, "How did I make this prediction?" or "Why did I infer here?" In this close study of the reading process, Kristi realized that understanding a book wasn't "you get it or you don't," but rather made up of a million complex processes that we are only slightly aware of as adults. When Kristi looked back with that lens, she realized she had known that guy would be trouble because he entered the scene at a suspicious time with knowledge he should not have had. Taking it one step further, she realized she could teach "Readers keep an eye out for characters that don't seem to belong and ask, 'Why is this character in this part?'" Often we talk about the writing process, but all of learning can be broken down into discrete replicable tasks. Early in her days at Teachers College, Kristi learned this as a "what/by/why," which is an overly simplistic way to get at task analysis . . . but a way that still works.

Think about *what* you want to teach. Now try to name the steps in how to do it anywhere—that is your *by*. Your *why* gives the reason you do that thing. To take a totally silly example: Let us teach you how to floss. To floss (what), you put the string in between your teeth and wrap it toward one tooth. Start at the top and pull down. Then put it back between the same teeth and wrap it toward the other tooth and pull down. Now repeat for the next set of teeth (by). This motion gets more plaque around the edges and prevents you from pushing

it into your gums (why). Not everything can be easily broken down, but everything does have a process you can dig out with the help of colleagues. And we emphasize process because you can use a process again and again. You can cycle back and make a process more sophisticated or tweak aspects. A process gets you a product, but making a product does not always teach you the process (just like the dentist flossing your teeth at an appointment does not mean you do it right at home).

Brad Stulberg (2016), in his article about why a total focus on product goals can backfire, suggests we increase the focus on the process instead: "First, set a goal. Next, figure out the steps to achieving that goal that are within your control. Then (mostly) forget about the goal, and focus on nailing the steps instead . . . A process mind-set creates daily opportunities for little victories, which help sustain the motivation required to accomplish long-term goals." Seeing instruction this way allows for much

PRODUCT

greater flexibility within our teaching. Instead of teaching children the goal is to solve this set of math problems correctly using this one algorithm, we can teach a series of processes for solving math problems that allow children to find their own personal path and celebrate small victories on the way to bigger goals.

Kids Need to Move It (Move It!)

Kristi has been writing in this section for the past forty-five minutes. In that time she has:

- ★ checked the mailbox
- ★ gotten two glasses of water
- ★ moved a plant to see if it looked better on the left of the counter
- ★ turned on a light
- ★ turned off a light
- ★ walked to the window.

While sitting and typing, she has rocked her body from side to side, bounced her knee up and down, and moved seating positions almost nonstop. If she were in a classroom where "sitting still" was a highly valued trait, she would have been in the principal's office a long time ago.

The fact of the matter is that human beings need to move. Children need to move even more. Why? Because they are hardwired to prioritize building automaticity in movement—this is often referred to as "muscle memory" and means that the movement comes to you automatically. A task that seems straightforward to us as adults, such as holding a pencil, is a movement that many children are still learning and so that's what the brain will focus on. Gill Connell and Cheryl McCarthy, authors of *A Moving Child is a Learning Child*, say it this way: "The human brain is *incapable* of doing more than one *thinking* task at a time. But it *can* layer one thinking task on top of one or more automated tasks" (2013, 24). We all have experience with this. Think of a Zumba class or a new workout you tried. It was nearly impossible to do the movements and think about work at the same time. As you learn the movements, and they become automatic, you are then able to think about what you want to make for dinner or what you need to do the next day while still following along.

If I am still learning how to move, I can't yet think deep thoughts and move at the same time. But eventually, when things like pencil grip become automatic, I can easily hold a pencil and stretch out the word *banana* simultaneously. Children are in the "learning how to move" state nearly constantly and are being driven by this lower part of their brain. And, as Connell and McCarthy say, "In short, when the brain is confronted with having to choose, it always prioritizes from the bottom up" (2013, 24). Meaning, no matter how engaging your lesson and how thoughtful your plans, a child's brain has already made a choice: movement first, academic tasks second.

And for many of us, movement is a far more natural state than sitting still. Have you ever tried to meditate? Christine will be the first to tell you that only when you try not to fidget can you understand how powerful the urge to fidget is. She's also the first to whip out a pad of paper at a faculty meeting to start doodling to help maintain focus. Movement is not counterproductive to learning; research has found the exact opposite is true! Moving helps you learn and how much you move predicts how you learn. Katrina Schwartz (2015) in her

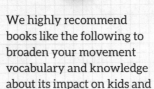

We highly recommend books like the following to broaden your movement vocabulary and knowledge about its impact on kids and learning:

- ❤ *A Moving Child Is a Learning Child: How the Body Teaches the Brain to Think* by Gill Connell and Cheryl McCarthy (201t3)

- ❤ *Big Body Play: Why Boisterous, Vigorous, and Very Physical Play Is Essential to Children's Development and Learning* by Frances M. Carlson (2011)

- ❤ *Math on the Move: Engaging Students in Whole Body Learning* by Malke Rosenfeld (2016)

TIP!

Look through your daily schedule. When do children have opportunities to move? Where can you build more time in? Can you make movement easier in the classroom through materials like bouncy chairs, small trampolines, floor cycles, or a station in the room for dance parties?

article "Why Kids Need to Move, Touch and Experience to Learn" cites the following study findings: "Researchers are studying the body movements of children as young as four-to-six months old and have found earlier and more frequent movement correlates with academic learning down the road. Kids who could sit up, sustain 'tummy time' longer and walk were all correlated with future academic success, even when researchers controlled for socioeconomics, family education and type of future education, among other mitigating factors." If you would like the magical solution to having a happy, joyful, productive classroom, it is this: give kids lots of opportunities to move. Have kids move when they are learning by acting out and gesturing; move when they are working by bouncing and standing and walking; move in loud, big ways to get gross motor skills developed; move in slow controlled ways to build self-regulation skills.

The better you build your schedule, the better your classroom will run. The more choice, agency, and balance you can put into it, the more likely that you will avoid the common problems of fatigue, frustration, and fidgets that can seem like larger behavior problems. A well-planned day—planned with children's unique needs in mind, that is—means fewer headaches for everyone later.

TYPES OF MOVEMENT

Body breaks quick bursts of movement that help you recenter and focus: bear crawls, movements that cross the midline, jumps on a small trampoline	GOOD FOR	individual children who need more movement opportunities, or for whom movement provides a way to refocus and concentrate
Incorporated movement small ways to imbed movement into your lessons ("If you think the character would do X, move to this side of the rug," "Let's all draw a big letter *B* in the air as Sara writes it on the chart.")	GOOD FOR	whole-class settings to engage all children in a physical way, teaching through movement
Big body play rough and tumble and physical play: tag, "superhero" play, running up the slide, loud, big play	GOOD FOR	*everyone!* Allows for social bonding, unstructured time to reboot, big, active movements and gross motor development
Organized movement games Simon Says, Duck Duck Goose, Red Light Green Light, Go Noodle videos, yoga	GOOD FOR	building self-control and following rules, gross motor development
Movement supports bouncy chairs, standing desks, hand fidgets, bubble seats, rocking chairs	GOOD FOR	anyone who moves as part of their thinking process; builds core strength, keeps fidgety kids more safely engaged in movement

Goodness-of-Fit

There is an idea in education that for children to develop most fully, they need to be in an environment that is well matched to their social, emotional, academic, and physical needs. This is known as "goodness of fit" (Wardle 2016). On an intuitive level, this makes sense to all of us who have been in a learning situation that did not feel "right" to us. Perhaps we withdrew, or our minds wandered. How can someone thrive when they are not seen and honored and educated as the person they are? We are the tailors and the carpenters who ensure a goodness of fit in our classrooms for each child by changing what we can and should about the school program. Classrooms can't be like stores that only carry certain clothing sizes, catering to the lucky few who fit into them. Instead, they must be like boutiques and design studios, cutting the cloth and shaping it to each client. This is not to say we should not have expectations, but that our expectations are rooted in the real science of child development and the day-to-day behavior we observe in our children. To expect all four-year-olds to sit and work quietly at a table for forty minutes on the first day of school is a recipe for disaster. We suggest looking at your schedule and the expectations for time spent, time between movement breaks, expectations for talking, expectations for social skills, and expectations for just about everything and ask, "Is this reflective of what I know about children? About development? About what I have observed?" If that question leaves you shrugging your shoulders and thinking *I don't know*, you are not alone. But! Good news! There are resources available in the world to help you!

- ♥ *Yardsticks: Children in the Classroom Ages 4-14* by Chip Wood (2007) lays out what is reasonable to expect at every age in terms of academics, social skills, and behavior based on child development.

- ♥ *The Whole-Brain Child: 12 Revolutionary Strategies to Nurture Your Child's Developing Mind* by Daniel Siegel and Tina Payne Bryson (2012) takes a close look at how children's brains are wired and offers specific strategies for how to foster emotional development.

- ♥ *Classroom Management Matters: The Social-Emotional Learning Approach Children Deserve* by Gianna Cassetta and Brook Sawyer (2015) breaks down how skills like self-regulation and relationships develop over the K–5 years.

Read these books! Study children! Ask questions! Kristi's expectations of kindergarteners shifted dramatically over the course of her years teaching the same grade and from the things she learned from others.

TIPS FOR MANAGING *YOUR* TIME AND SCHEDULE

→ Find when you do you best work and develop a habit of getting as much as you can done then. Some teachers come in early in the morning to prep for the day, and others stay into the evening. Some teachers wake up early on Sunday morning, and others work after dinner.

→ Keep a running "do now" and "do soon" list. Triage what needs to get done immediately (grab that library book before read-aloud!) and what can wait (we're looking at you, papers to file . . .).

→ Set boundaries with your email and communicate them clearly to parents. It's OK to say that you don't check email from 4:00 p.m. to 7:30 a.m. The world will keep turning. And stick to those boundaries—give yourself some time to recharge.

→ Establish routines for when you tackle certain tasks such as writing your class newsletter (every Friday at prep!) or responding to emails (before the day starts and right after dismissal!) and stick to them.

Annotated Schedules

Next, you will find schedules from actual classrooms and actual teachers. These are not meant to be set in stone, but rather give you a sense of how some teachers navigate the complexities of the demands placed on them by their school and the real needs of the students in front of them.

Kindergarten Weekly Schedule

This is Kristi's classroom schedule from one year. It tends to look different year after year as she tries new things out. She is required to have reading, writing, math, inquiry, and choice time in her schedule. Prep periods (in green) are also assigned. Timing and placement is left to her discretion. One tip when making a schedule is to think across your whole week. Math may be shortened one day, but lengthened the next. Consider what needs to happen daily and what can happen a few

	MONDAY	TUESDAY	WEDNESDAY
8:45–8:55	Morning work choice · Sensory bins · Word-study activities · Reading · Book making · Math bins	Morning work choice · Sensory bins · Word-study activities · Reading · Book making · Math bins	Morning work choice · Sensory bins · Word-study activities · Reading · Book making · Math bins
8:55–9:15	Meeting · Shared reading · Word study · Read-aloud	Meeting · Shared reading · Word study · Read-aloud	Meeting · Shared reading · Word study · Read-aloud
9:15–10:20	Work time Reading/Writing workshops Break/Snack as needed	Work time Reading/Writing workshops Break/Snack as needed	Work time Reading/Writing workshops Break/Snack as needed
10:20–11:10	Choice time	Choice time	Choice time
11:10–12:15	Lunch and recess	Lunch and recess	Lunch and recess
12:15–1:05	Art	Meeting 12:15–12:30 · SE skills/Whole-class talk · Math routines Math stations 12:30–1:05	Meeting 12:15–12:30 · SE skills/Whole-class talk · Math routines Math stations 12:30–1:05
	Meeting 1:10–1:20 · SE skills/Whole-class talk · Math routines Math stations 1:20–2:00	Gym 1:10–2:00	Music 1:10–2:00
2:00–2:40	Inquiry	Inquiry	Inquiry
2:40–2:50	Read-aloud/Snack Gratitude circle	Read-aloud/Snack Gratitude circle	Read-aloud/Snack Gratitude circle

This time, though spent on the rug, has movement incorporated throughout.

SE skills stands for Social Emotional skills. At this time, Kristi does much of the work laid out in *A Mindset for Learning* to reflect and build active learning stances.

times a week. Since this is kindergarten, times are shorter. There is no forty-five minute writing block, especially in the fall. Once the year progresses, there may be days when writing extends to forty-five minutes because the work is on fire, but other days it might get fifteen minutes because there is a big math project happening. It is what happens over all 180+ days that ultimately matters, not one random Tuesday.

THURSDAY	FRIDAY
Morning work choice · Sensory bins · Word-study activities · Reading · Book making · Math bins	Morning work choice · Sensory bins · Word-study activities · Reading · Book making · Math bins
Meeting · Shared reading · Word study · Read-aloud	Meeting · Shared reading · Word study · Read-aloud
Work time Reading/Writing workshops Break/Snack as needed	Work time Reading/Writing workshops Break/Snack as needed
Choice time	Library
Lunch and recess	Lunch and recess
Meeting 12:15–12:30 · SE skills/Whole-class talk · Math routines	Meeting 12:15–12:30 · SE skills/Whole-class talk · Math routines
Math stations 12:30–1:05	Math stations 12:30–1:05
Social circle 1:10–2:00	Book buddies 1:10–2:00
Inquiry	Choice time
Read-aloud/Snack Gratitude circle	Read-aloud/Snack Gratitude circle

This is an open-ended block of time for kids to choose activities. Sensory bins include things like water beads, play doh, and sand. The only materials off limits at this time are large blocks and dramatic play materials. The list of activities was developed through whole-class conversation.

Work time allows children to select whether to read books or make books as Kristi pulls small groups in reading and writing. Children are working within a workshop approach (See Section 3) but it is not until later in the year that Kristi begins a more formal reading and writing workshop. Break is integrated within this time, about midway through, and children eat snack when they feel hungry.

Math stations allow for small-group direct instruction, while other children are tackling investigations or playing math games. This creates more choice than traditional math structures.

Gratitude circle incorporates storytelling and reflection about the best parts of the day.

First-Grade Weekly Schedule

This is a schedule from one of Christine's years teaching first grade. Christine's math and reading blocks were scheduled for her and interventionists arrived at set times to run small groups and support students. Much as in Kindergarten, the first graders started the year with much shorter blocks of structured time and much longer blocks of unstructured time, and

	MONDAY	TUESDAY	WEDNESDAY
8:10–8:30	Morning meeting · Number talk · Community conversation · Shared reading	Morning meeting · Number talk · Community conversation · Shared reading	Morning meeting · Number talk · Community conversation · Shared reading
8:30–9:10	Choice time	Choice time	Choice time
9:10–9:15	9:00–9:45 Reading workshop (Interventionist: 9:00–9:30)	Transition to art	Transition to music
9:15–9:55	9:45–10:00 Snack and transition to art	9:15–9:55 Art	9:15–9:55 Music
9:55–10:15		Transition and snack	Transition and snack
10:15–10:55	Art	Reading workshop (Interventionist 10:15–10:45)	Reading workshop (Interventionist 10:15–10:45)
10:55–11:05	Outside break	Outside break	Outside break
11:05–11:20	Word work	Read-aloud	Word work
11:20–12:00	Writing workshop	Writing workshop	Writing workshop
12:00–12:30	Recess	Recess	Recess
12:35–1:05	Lunch	Lunch	Lunch
1:10–2:00	Math (Interventionist 1:15–1:45)	Math (Interventionist 1:15–1:45)	Math (Interventionist 1:15–1:45)
2:00–2:15	Snack/Break		Snack/Break
	Read-aloud		Read-aloud
2:15–2:35	Science/Social studies		Science/Social studies
2:35–2:50	Closing circle/Storytelling Interactive writing	Early release (2:00)	Closing circle/Storytelling Interactive writing

Every Tuesday the students would leave an hour early and the faculty would meet for professional development.

then those times gradually expanded to the schedule below. Christine decided to start the day—after a quick meeting—with choice time so that the children could settle into school and make choices about how they wanted to start their days.

THURSDAY	FRIDAY
Morning meeting · Number talk · Community conversation · Shared reading	Morning meeting · Number talk · Community conversation · Shared reading
Choice time	Choice time
Transition to PE	Transition to PE
9:15–9:55 PE	9:15–9:55 PE
Transition and snack	Transition and snack
Reading workshop (Interventionist 10:00–10:30)	Reading workshop (Interventionist 10:15–10:45)
10:45–11:25 Music–Diana	Outside break
	Word work
Writing workshop	Writing workshop
Recess	Recess
Lunch	Lunch
Math (Interventionist 1:15–1:45)	Math (Interventionist 1:15–1:45)
Snack/Break	Snack/Break
Read-aloud	Read-aloud
Science/Social studies	Science/Social studies
Closing circle/Storytelling Interactive writing	Closing circle/Storytelling Interactive writing

The set recess and lunch times were augmented by additional outside times and snacks when needed. Christine's class got very skilled at speedily putting on winter layers to fit in the quick outside play breaks, even when the weather was less than ideal.

In the beginning of the year the math block started with unstructured math manipulative centers or games where students could explore and transition back from lunch.

Christine alternated science and social studies units every six weeks or so.

Third-Grade Weekly Schedule

This schedule comes courtesy of the third-grade teaching team of Kathryn Cazes and Molly Murray. These two teachers work in an Integrated Coteaching Classroom (ICT) which means the classroom has two full-time teachers—one general education certified and one special education certified. The class itself is comprised of a mix of children with individualized education plans (IEPS) and without. Due to the coteaching arrangement, this schedule has some unique characteristics. In stations, each teacher teaches a specific lesson and children rotate through. Children are heterogeneously grouped. A stop at each station can be short (ten minutes or so)

	MONDAY	TUESDAY
Notes:		
		Parent engagement
1st Period 8:40–9:30	Unpack/Jobs Math	Unpack/Jobs Math
2nd Period 9:35–10:25	Music	Gym
3rd Period 10:30–11:20	Stations: Group 1–Writing workshop Group 2–Reading workshop Group 3–Extra recess and word study	Stations: Group 3–Writing workshop Group 1–Reading workshop Group 2–Extra recess and word study
4th Period 11:20–12:10	Lunch and roof	Lunch and roof
5th Period 12:15–1:05	Copy homework Read-aloud Social Studies	Copy homework Read-aloud Buddies
6th Period 1:10–2:00	Stations: Group 2–Writing workshop Group 3–Reading workshop Group 1–Extra recess and word study	Stations: Group 1–Writing workshop Group 2–Reading workshop Group 3–Extra recess (Marcia) and word study
7th Period 2:05–2:55	Stations: Group 3–Writing workshop Group 1–Reading workshop Group 2–Extra recess and word study	Stations: Group 2–Writing workshop Group 3–Reading workshop Group 1–Extra recess

or long (forty-five minutes to an hour). As you look at the schedule you may notice names or the phrase "push in." This is in reference to service providers like speech or occupational therapists who come into the classroom and support the students. To avoid the sense that certain teachers only work with certain children, groups are mixed constantly throughout the day, rarely in homogeneous ways. Almost every academic subject is taught in small station groups, and you will see ample time for movement and an additional focus on social skills.

WEDNESDAY	THURSDAY	FRIDAY
Other professional		
Unpack/Jobs Stations: Group 2–Writing workshop Group 3–Reading workshop Group 1–Extra recess	Unpack/Jobs Math	Unpack/Jobs Math
Library Grade-level planning	9:20–10:00 Read-aloud/Social studies 10:00–11:00 Social stations · Friend files · Skill streaming · Grand conversation	Reading workshop
Technology Ends 1/11	10:00–11:00 Social stations Friend files (Johanna push in) Social secrets (Skill streaming) Grand conversation/Talk moves 11:00–11:20 Word study	Science
Lunch and roof	Lunch and roof	Lunch and roof
Read-aloud 12:50–1:20 Math	Reading workshop	12:15–12:45 Social studies 12:45–1:20 Writing workshop
Stations: Group 3–Writing workshop Group 1–Reading workshop Group 2–Extra recess and word study	1:10–2:05 Art	1:25–2:00 Choice time
Stations: Group 1–Writing workshop Group 2–Reading workshop Group 3–Extra recess (Marcia) and word study	Writing workshop	Chess Ends 1/20

Fifth-Grade Weekly Schedule

This schedule comes courtesy of Anna Bennett, fifth-grade teacher extraordinaire. Anna is a winner of a Big Apple Teaching Award in New York City, a prestigious award granted to just fifteen teachers in the NYC area.

When asked to talk a bit about her schedule, Anna said, "With such a packed schedule (and—awesome—extracurriculars like chess and Creative Stages popping up at different times of the year), it can be hard to fit in time for reading workshop, writing workshop and math workshop each day. When I create my schedule, I plot in those blocks of time first and

	START	MONDAY	TUESDAY
1st Period 8:40–9:30	8:40	Unpack and extra recess	Music
	8:50		
	9:05	Reading workshop	
	9:15		
2nd Period 9:35–10:25	9:35	Math workshop	Morning routine
	9:45		Math workshop
	10:00		
3rd Period 10:30–11:20		Gym (Common plan)	Coteaching Reading workshop
4th Period 11:20–12:10	11:25	Read-aloud	Coteaching Writing workshop
	11:45	2nd-grade reading buddies	
5th Period 12:15–1:05	12:15	Recess and lunch	Recess and lunch
6th Period 1:10–2:00	1:10	Coteaching Writing workshop	Read-aloud
	1:25		Word study
	1:45		
7th Period 2:05–2:55	2:05	Coteaching Grand conversation	Technology
	2:35		
	2:45	Closing meeting	

Anna's class has a large percentage of students with IEPs and therefore has a coteaching period with a special education teacher every day.

Grand conversation is a teaching structure that involves the whole class engaging in discourse around a topic. This could be inquiry related to a read-aloud, or general classroom issues.

work from there. In fifth grade, we officially have one full block of choice time each week where kids work on proposals, projects, inquiries, etc. However, that doesn't quite feel like enough play, so we also fit in two extra recess sessions each week (and use the inquiry room for our social studies work). Fitting in read-aloud, social studies, word study and buddies, then, is just about being creative and being efficient with time. My kids and I talk a lot at the beginning of the year about being efficient with transitions so that we can get to more each day, and that really helps fit in a few different areas of study within one period of time."

WEDNESDAY	THURSDAY	FRIDAY
Morning routine	Morning routine	
Read-aloud	Word study	Art
Extra recess	Social studies	
Coteaching Reading workshop	Science	Morning routine
		Word study
		Read-aloud/ Social studies
Coteaching Reading workshop	Coteaching Reading workshop	Coteaching Reading workshop
Science	Coteaching Reading workshop	Coteaching Reading workshop
Recess and lunch	Recess and lunch	Recess and lunch
Math workshop	Read-aloud	Math workshop
Social studies	Math workshop	Choice time
Word study		
Closing meeting	Closing meeting	Closing meeting

The inquiry room is a room with blocks, art materials, and open spaces for children to build and recreate what they are learning (for example, making the ships the explorers sailed on). The key to the inquiry room is that children are selecting the questions and materials they want to study while in that space.

Choice time refers to an open block where children can work with blocks and art materials, create dramatic stories, or just play.

Big Idea: Build a Community, Don't Just Manage One

If there is one thing we have come to realize in our collected years of teaching, it is that building a productive, functional, joyful community of unique individuals is harder than anyone realizes. Sometimes it feels darn near impossible. But the truth is, it does not matter how well you teach reading, or math, or how beautiful your inquiry question is—if your classroom is in chaos, no learning will happen. All teachers have experienced chaos. Most teachers have "The Story." For Kristi, it was looking up from a small group to see that her independent readers were not reading and using Post-its for great thinking, they were actually launching said Post-its in balls out of her third-floor window. For Christine, it was turning around from zipping up a jacket to see a full-fledged game of tag happening across chairs and table tops. The hardest and rawest truth is that this lack of classroom harmony is never the kids' fault, any more than their progress (or lack thereof) in reading and math is their fault. These issues are the domain of teaching. Chaos does not come to order through wishing it so, nor does it come from not smiling until October; it comes from empathy and time, and a teacher working thoughtfully and relentlessly toward it.

The term *classroom management* is often used by schools to refer to the process of affecting the state of the classroom community. This phrase has never sat particularly well with us, perhaps because this is how *Oxford Living Dictionaries* defines *management*: "the process of dealing with or controlling things or people" (https://en.oxforddictionaries.com/definition/management). To put that phrase alongside living, breathing children feels icky to us. You manage your money. You manage your "to file" pile (or not), but we don't believe you "manage" developing human beings. There is a reason our title is *teacher* and not *manager*.

We teach our children how to exist in a community unlike one they have ever seen before. We teach them how to resolve disputes with others who are different from them. We teach them how to demonstrate empathy and compassion, and how to handle disappointments. And when we are open, we realize that our children are teaching us what it means to be a four-, six-, or ten-year-old in the world now, which is infinitely different from the world we grew up in.

Defining the Difference Between Classroom Management and Classroom Community

There are many, many ways to achieve an orderly, well-functioning classroom, but we do not believe all of them are created equal. Just because something can work, does not mean it is ethically the best choice for the world. We could throw out a yogurt container in the trash, rather than rinsing it and placing it in the recycling bin, but that is a short-term benefit (saving a few seconds) with long-term, cumulative damage (see you later Antarctic ice cap!). To our thinking, more traditional classroom management moves may seem effective in the short term, but carry a long-term cost.

So what do we mean when we say *management*? And what do we wish schools were saying instead? Well, here is our attempt to define this:

Classroom Management: A short-term control-based solution that often relies on punishments and rewards in lieu of teaching an alternate behavior.

Community Building: The thoughtful, long-term teaching, modeling, and habit building of prosocial, positive behaviors (e.g., listening, resolving disputes with others, listening to others' points of view) and productive habits of mind (e.g., flexibility, resilience, empathy).

For too long, schools have emphasized management over instruction-based community building. This works on the assumption that children *know* how to act as part of a community and choose to do so, or not to do so. In our experience, this is a false assumption. Children show us what they understand constantly, and what can look like misbehavior is most likely a child's best approximation of the skill we are asking for: listening, sharing, problem solving, and so on. And when it is not a child's best approximation, it is usually a child trying to tell us something we aren't hearing any other way. This is not to say that you will never, ever, ever use a classroom management strategy. We would be lying if we said that we have never used call-and-response or tacked a silly reward on to facilitate a fast cleanup. What we would say is that classroom management options should be used sparingly, if it all, and the bulk of your work to achieve classroom harmony should be around building a community through the explicit teaching of social skills (more on that in the next section!).

People of the World, the Real World: Authentic and Reasonable Community Expectations

Just as when teaching reading or math we try to identify an authentic skill or objective, we do the same in building community. We hold onto the idea that there is some skill or objective the classroom community needs to acquire because it will help children in the classroom and *in the world*. It may even help to name your objective for "people in the world," rather than "my students" to help separate your fantasy classroom desires from what the world *actually* needs. Your objective will probably not be something like "I want my students to do everything I say" because, when reworded, "I want *people of the world* to do everything I say" makes you sound like a crazy dictator. However, an objective like "*People of the world* should listen to each other respectfully" sounds like something worth teaching.

POSSIBLE OBJECTIVE	MANAGEMENT OPTION	COMMUNITY-BUILDING OPTION
A WAY TO GET EVERY PERSON'S ATTENTION IN LARGE SETTINGS	Call-and-response ("Stop, look, and listen"; "OK!") If we *only* use this option, we lose the chance to teach into the skills of speaking and listening that govern conversations.	Teach children that when they hear a voice to stop and listen closely (like we do when the pilot speaks on an airplane). Plan to say the most important thing second because by then the chatter will have ceased.
PRODUCTIVE WORK TIMES	Assigned seats/line spots/rug spots If we *only* use this option, children will not develop an understanding of themselves as a student and a learner, and could become dependent on a teacher for self-management.	Teach what it means to choose a productive spot; expect children will try out lots of spots before they find one that works for their body and way of working (more on flexible seating in the physical environment section on page 50).
KINDNESS	Filling buckets, compliment jars, stickers If we *only* use this option, children may develop a "What do I get if I . . ." mentality toward kindness and compassion.	Teach what empathy and compassion are; role-play and develop guidelines for demonstrating these things. Reflect on how they feel and how they help the community.
PEOPLE APPLYING THEIR "BEST EFFORT" TO WORK	Awarding stickers or prizes for work being "the best" If we *only* use this option, we run the risk of effort being tied to approval from others, and orient people toward a fixed mindset.	Teach what effort feels like; demonstrate the self-talk and body language consistent with effort. Ask children to self-evaluate their own effort.
SELF-REGULATION	Clip charts, color charts, etc., for demonstrations of obedience and to "prompt" kids into behavioral changes This option often creates the myth of the "bad kid" and does not teach self-management strategies (nor does it allow for the reality that all of us run into issues socially and behaviorally).	Teach self-regulation strategies and techniques and practice them daily. Self-regulation is a muscle that, like any other, can be made stronger with support. For more on self-regulation, see "Supporting Every Child" on page 93. 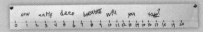

But What If No One Listens to Me?!

OK, so, you threw out the clip chart; vowed to not use "stop, look, and listen"; and stuck the stickers in the art center and the treasure chest in the dress up area. Good for you! But then, you look around your room and it feels like chaos. There are a few things that will help you.

Set Clear Expectations with Your Children

Don't assume every child knows how a school community works. Spend time in collaborative conversations to talk about how the kiddos want the classroom to run. Establish a few bottom lines to be guides in how the community will act.

> **Gather your class together.** Set the tone for these conversations by having your class sit in a circle at a time of day (morning meeting, just after read aloud) when students are fresh and ready to collaborate.

> **Reflect on a positive experience.** Hold the conversations after a harmonious whole-class activity such as choice time or a game of tag. Ask, "What went well?" "Why did it go well?"

> **Use positive language.** "Don't hit" is not as useful an expectation as "Use a safe body with friends and with materials."

> **Circle back to the expectations often.** Return to these conversations and your class expectations often, revising and adding to them as you need to. Use the phrase *People of the world* as a litmus test.

The Responsive Classroom book *The First Six Weeks of School* (2015) recommends having these conversations in the first few days of school. Check out that book for more resources on these conversations.

Then Act Out, Role-Play, and Further Define Those Expectations

Everyone can set intentions; think about how many times you have claimed you are going to get in shape, eat more kale, file your papers on the day you use them—meeting expectations is the hard part. Building habits can take between 50 and 264 days (Dean 2013). Think of your expectations as habits you want children to build, and that will take time. How do you build a habit? Intentional and sustained practice until it becomes an action without conscious thought. Defining terms like *a safe and unsafe body*, *listening*, or *respect*, then practicing those things, is no different than how we teach anything else. This is the step we most often miss when teaching social skills.

Make A Plan (Not a Punishment) When Expectations Are Not Met

To build a habit, you need to build a neural pathway. Sometimes you need to deconstruct an old neural pathway (I am angry so I hit) before building the new one. Punishment doesn't really play a role in that cycle. Our friend and colleague, Shanna Schwartz, from Teachers College Reading and Writing Project said to us, "If a child is having the same issue again and again, we have to consider if we have made a plan *with* the child to do something different." Just punishing doesn't set up for an alternate behavior.

For more resources on building classroom communities check out:

- ❤ Responsive Classroom (responsiveclassroom.org)
- ❤ Center for the Collaborative Classroom (collaborativeclassroom.org)
- ❤ Social Thinking (socialthinking.com)
- ❤ Restorative Justice (restorativejustice.org)

Sadly, it can't always be as simple as "When you are mad, use your words." That is not how anger is managed in the real world. Think of when you are angry—really, really angry. Kristi has to go for a run. Christine needs to spend time alone and write. We have learned socially acceptable ways to manage our anger, and rarely is it to immediately engage in civilized discourse. Sit with the child and ask, "What does anger feel like? How do you know when you are angry? Where in your body do you feel your anger? Show me with your hands how big you're feeling your anger." Once a child can identify that feeling, we need to substitute the action for something more socially adept. Rather than hitting when angry, stomping three times can release some of that emotion, or maybe pushing the wall as hard as you can for thirty seconds. This child might be quite capable of using her words once she gets a physical outlet for her anger.

Getting punished for being angry and hitting isn't entirely fair or helpful. It often just isolates a child without giving him a chance to learn how to exist better in the world. We would never take a book away every time a reader missed a word—we teach strategies to manage the tricky parts.

When a child breaks a community expectation, she should spend some time repairing that break. Consequences, in this sense, should be something that you do *for* someone or something (your community, the person you hurt), not something that is taken away (choice time, recess). Author and education expert Alfie Kohn warns that consequences are often just punishments in disguise. And punishments, he writes, erode the relationships between teachers and students: "Kids need to be able to develop trusting relationships with adults. . . . power-based interactions between teachers and kids (such as punishment) fundamentally disrupt that trust and any sort of caring alliance. The tougher the kid, the more critical it is to establish that alliance—and thus, paradoxically, the more important it is not to punish when the kid does something wrong" (Meier 2013).

So what does that repair work look like in a community? If you hurt someone, physically or emotionally, you need to try to fix that to the best of your ability. For a first grader, that might be writing a letter of apology and acting out how to solve the problem differently. For an older student, that might look like a restorative justice circle. If you decide to draw on the table in magic marker, even though you know that is not how to handle materials, you need to fix that too. We continue to use the real world as our touchstone—when we send an email we instantly regret or back into another car, we don't immediately retreat into a time-out, we work to repair our mistakes and (hopefully) learn from them. The same is true for children—it is not about punishment, it is about the logical consequence of your actions and learning ways to change your actions to avoid similar situations in the future.

WE INTERRUPT THIS BROADCAST FOR SOME REAL TALK

Everyone is their best teacher version before the kids arrive. But afterward, you are likely to get frustrated and do something or say something that you wish you could take back the moment it occurs. We have all been there. Here are some tips to keep you from going back:

→ Know your triggers. If interrupting (for example) is your kryptonite, know that. Just knowing that gets under your skin will help you manage your reactions and more often keep your cool.

→ Sing when you want to yell. This is advice almost every primary teacher gets and it really works. No one lining up? Start singing about how its line-up time and, like the Pied Piper, kids will follow what you say. It also will likely make you feel ridiculous and therefore make you realize lining up is not life and death.

→ Get some space. We often teach kids to take space: do the same for yourself. It's OK to tell children, "I need a moment before I can talk to you about this." Then do what you need to do to get recentered and be the best version of you.

→ If you mess up (and you will), own up to it. Say, "I am sorry I yelled about the mess. I was feeling frustrated that no one was cleaning up. What can we do to make sure clean up goes better tomorrow?"

At the End of the Day

Part of our job is to be calm, happy people. That seems like such a simple thing, but when a community is having a hard time coming together, it is easy to slip into behaviors that run counter to how we would want our community to run. A classroom run on fear or shame does not teach how to live boldly and kindly in the world. Expect a little chaos; expect kids will be silly and noisy and some will hit and some will interrupt. Be thankful when no one bites, and when they do, know that you can help them learn better ways to communicate. Community building, like all teaching, is slow and steady, but so is the act of growing into a compassionate and critical thinker. Management will get you compliance, but it won't get you community. You need to teach social skills for that.

Big Idea: Social Skills Can Be Taught

In the past, maybe even when you were in school, the assumption was that social skills were something you had or you didn't have, sort of like being born with a certain color hair. Kids were bad or good. Behavior was rewarded or punished. You probably remember some of these things: tickets and class stores, marble parties, timeouts, and notes home that had to be signed. You might remember some of the rewards favorably (that pizza party!) but you might still also cringe with shame over that punishment (you didn't mean to talk during silent reading, why did you have to write a note to your grown-up that said you did?). The question for us as educators is, did it work? Did we become better community members and better people because of the pizza parties and the time-outs?

Research suggests probably not. Katherine Reynolds Lewis, in her article "What If Everything You Knew About Discipline Was Wrong?" writes "Contemporary psychological studies suggest that, far from resolving children's behavior problems, these standard disciplinary methods often exacerbate them" (2015). Color charts, clip charts, tickets, and stickers cause more problems than they solve because they don't address the core issue. Social skills have to be learned, not just enforced. Lewis asks this question in her article: "Are we treating chronically misbehaving children as though they don't want to behave, when in many cases they simply *can't*?" It is essential to reframe your view of behavior as a series of learned skills, much like you may see reading or math. What you see in front of you is what children have learned about existing in a community. Just as children may overrely on sounding out in reading when they arrive at your door, children may have learned social skills that aren't universally helpful. Skills that help you navigate your family and your community may not serve the same beneficial purpose in school. So, if a child does not yet know how to be successful in school, what do we do? We teach them how.

Social skills can be taught, just like reading skills or math skills. Kids enter schools with differing experiences in academic domains, and it is our job as teachers to assess and teach the necessary skills for success. The same is true for social skills. But how? Often we hear teachers say that they want their students to be respectful, but respect is really many skills such as listening, following directions, sharing, and turn taking. The first step is seeing a social skill like we see an academic skill: something that can be broken down into several discrete, teachable steps. There are many resources to help you with this (*Skillstreaming the Elementary School Child* by Dr. Ellen McGinnis [2011] is among the most complete), but it is also something you can puzzle out with colleagues or the children in your classroom. In fact, engaging children in your classroom in each of the questions we pose models the important skills of self-reflection and problem solving. Children bring myriad kinds of expertise to the classroom, and asking for their help and thoughts demonstrates the high value you place on their experience and ability to contribute meaningfully to the class community.

Sometimes as we work to break down social skills, we uncover our own hidden bias and assumptions about children's experiences. For example, we may assume children feel comfortable talking to adults or believe adults to be trustworthy. We may rely too much on our own experience growing up, or how we parent. In truth, we are all flawed, we all have room to learn, and we can all be better at our social interactions. Don't despair! Just as in all things, the more we listen, observe, and reflect, the better we will get at breaking skills down and teaching them to children.

Breaking Down a Skill: Sharing

Here is a typical classroom scenario, one that we have lived, most teachers have lived, and you might live in the next twenty-four hours.

If incidents like this keep occurring within the classroom, or with one child in particular, then you probably need to teach into the skill of sharing. It might sound silly, but ask yourself, "What experience have my students had with sharing?" Maybe they are only children who don't have siblings to squabble with? Maybe they come from a household where each child has his own of everything? Or maybe this child has never had a chance to have something of her own? In classrooms where supplies have been labeled with each child's name, sharing is rarely needed, and the skill may never have been taught. First, ground yourself in the mindset that if your kiddos could share, they would. Other questions you might ask yourself or your class to help address this (or any) issue might be:

What do we (my students and I) understand about this skill?

Is this skill important for people to be successful in life? Why?

What is hard about this skill?

What is reasonable for children of this age when it comes to this skill?

For many children, and adults if we are being honest, sharing means "I get it and you don't," and sometimes children (and adults) have learned this as a manipulation technique: "If I say you aren't sharing, I get it and I keep it." Sometimes it seems easier to just get two of everything or remove the high-demand object, but this is a short-term solution to a societal issue. Rather than contributing to a society of selfish hoarders, we are better off teaching the importance of, and strategies for, sharing anything.

For every skill that you'd like to teach, from sharing to waiting to dealing with disappointment, you can ask yourself this series of questions to help break down what you want to teach, how you will teach it and why it's important to teach:

⭐ What does this skill look like when it is done proficiently?

⭐ What are the steps involved?

⭐ What are the reasons this skill is beneficial to the people using it?

You may never have thought this out, so take a moment and try it here:

- What does sharing look like?
- What are the steps?
- Why should I bother?

You may have come up with something like:

What does sharing look like? Sharing looks like the passing off of, or splitting of, an item between two or more people in an equal way.

What are the steps? The steps might be something like:

1. Decide if the item needs to be shared, or if there is more than one that can be used.

2. Ask, "Who goes first? Who goes next?" (Tips: rock, paper, scissors; guess my number; letter of first name are all fair ways to decide who goes first.)

3. Make a plan: how much time/amount with item?

Why should I bother? And the reasons to bother sharing? It helps you make and keep friends. It allows everyone in the community access to cool things. It saves money. It helps the community.

Now What? Practice Makes Progress

Now it is time to teach the steps and practice them, like any other skill set. You can use the previous questions to design solutions to any issue or problem that comes up: hitting, interrupting, hiding during cleanup, gossiping, whatever. Even more importantly, you send a message of growth and potential. There are no bad readers, bad writers, or bad kids. Period. We are all learning to be the best versions of ourselves, and school helps us do that.

How Do We Teach the Steps of Social Skills?

Option 1: Class Conversation and Reflection

First things first, you want to put this to the community. There is no benevolent dictatorship in your classroom; you are the lead learner and so begin that way! Research has found that "Learning is more effective if a lesson or experience is deliberately coupled with time spent thinking about what was just presented" (Fondas 2014). Taking the time to do this might feel stressful in light of all the other demands placed on you in the classroom, but remember, teaching is never about content alone. When you tackle a problem this way, you are teaching the intellectual skills of collaboration, analysis, questioning, clarity, active listening, and reflective thinking—skills that children will use every day of their thinking lives.

How Does Whole-Class Conversation Work in the Classroom?

Whole-class conversations are meant to be conversations between children, with the teacher serving as a rudder of sorts, directing toward key points as needed. More often than not, this conversation is launched with a question or a problem. Sometimes it is the teacher putting it out there, and other times it will come directly from students. Once the question or idea is out there, the conversation exists to problem solve. Children may or may not raise hands

Watch Kristi lead a conversation on what to do when someone says, "STOP!"

hein.pub/kidsfirst-login

keycode: KIDSFIRST2018

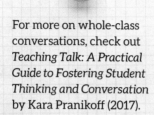

For more on whole-class conversations, check out *Teaching Talk: A Practical Guide to Fostering Student Thinking and Conversation* by Kara Pranikoff (2017).

(that is a classroom preference), but the key is that the children are talking to each other, not the teacher. The teacher may physically remove himself, lingering behind the students or taking a less obvious seat. The children may move into a circle shape so everyone can be seen. The teacher may pop into the conversation from time to time, but the bulk of the dialogue comes from students. Teachers may help address issues like taking turns or using questions to better understand another person's point. The social aspects of conversation—looking at the speaker, demonstrating active listening, using names—may also be points of instruction.

In the beginning, these conversations may feel chaotic, with a lot (or no) children talking, and the same idea being bandied around for five minutes. Don't despair! Keep having them, choosing one thing to teach or improve each time you gather for conversations. This can be one of the most impactful ways of building and sustaining your community over time.

Option 2: Read-Aloud and Storytelling

Storytelling is one of the most powerful tools we have for communicating and remembering information as human beings. As psychoanalyst Phillipa Perry wrote in *How to Stay Sane* (2012): "Our way of being in the world will . . . come from stories that we read and are told to us. . . ." (2012, 95). This is important to know because "our emotional, cognitive and physical response—that is, our typical pattern for dealing with recurrent situations—will come from our own stories" (95). Essentially, we tell stories to ourselves to make sense of what has happened to us, and then those stories, and the stories we read and hear, impact our future decisions, whether or not we are consciously aware of it.

This self-storytelling begins first in our families. Carlin Flora (2006), in her article "Self-Portrait in a Skewed Mirror," writes "In early childhood, we learn storytelling from our parents. Mothers and fathers who provide coherent, emotion-rich narratives of family life have children who develop more coherent narratives of their own life experience by the end of the preschool years, says Robin Fivush, professor of psychology at Emory University. (Such kids reap additional cognitive and social benefits from narrative wizardry, Fivush notes)." These narratives aren't necessarily dramatic acts of storytelling; instead, they're woven into the fabric of the child's day. From calmly and cheerfully helping children clean up a spill to noticing when they share something with a sibling, children are constructing stories about themselves and the world constantly; we can help children co-construct positive narratives that enable them to act in community-minded, empathic ways. The key here is co-construction. Engaging children in conversations around read-alouds, or having them help co-construct a story about certain behaviors, is what makes this powerful. It is not about lecturing at children, it is about engaging them in a process of problem solving and thoughtful discussion.

How Does Storytelling Sound in the Classroom?

When you craft a story to tell in the classroom, the more explicit the steps and thinking that led to success are made, the more children will see the blueprint to follow next time. A story that sounds like "and then they shared and everyone was happy" skates over the challenging aspects of sharing. If we are using storytelling to teach, we have to make sure the *how* is explicit. Otherwise it is like teaching reading by saying, "And then you read it. Good luck in life, kids!" This could sound like, "The two friends went to the share chart and decided it would be fair to use a timer to share the special train." We can use storytelling in visualization and role-play, but it can also be its own stand-alone structure.

How Does Read-Aloud Sound in the Classroom?

In an interactive read-aloud, stopping to ask questions and letting the children turn and talk to each other helps them understand different ways of being in the world. Just like in storytelling, read-alouds and the experiences of the characters serve as guides for when a child is in a similar situation or as a reflection on something that's happened in the past. Sometimes children find it easier to talk about difficult situations when they occur to characters rather than themselves or their classmates. Stop at key moments in the story and ask questions to elicit this kind of thinking, such as:

⭐ Why do you think the character just did that? Did that surprise you?

⭐ What could they have done instead?

⭐ If you were the character, what might you do next? Why?

⭐ What might the character do to solve this problem?

⭐ What could we learn from this story?

Option 3: Visualization and Role-Play

You know how when you watch Olympic skiers prepare for their turns, you see them mimicking the movements they will need to make with their eyes closed? Or how basketball players mime taking free throws before they actually shoot the ball? That is all visualization, and it works as well to build mental habits as it does physical ones. When we practice something again and again, even if it is just in our mind, it helps us to build a knowing network around that habit, which makes it more likely we act that way. Sunni Brown, in her book *The Doodle Revolution*, talks about it this way: "Our knowing network, you may suspect, is that circuit of connected, functional areas in the brain that gives us the feeling that we *know* something . . . we can strengthen our knowing networks around realities *that we want to bring to life*—and in doing so, directly impact our potential of moving toward those realities" (2014, 36).

When we role-play and visualize, it is like running mental shooting drills. We train our brain how to react in certain situations before we even get into them. Astronauts do it, pilots do it, sports players do it. And five-year-olds can do it too.

How Do Visualization and Role-Play Work in the Classroom?

Visualization and role-play can exist in a whole-class or one-on-one fashion, depending on the needs of the children. They are meant to be short and often need to be done repeatedly to make an impact on behavior. Visualization might involve children closing their eyes as you tell a story about the social skill you are working on, like sharing or listening. As you tell the story, possibly a real thing that happened, or one co-constructed with children, you are reinforcing the steps you have

Watch Kristi teach a small group that combines word study and social skills.

hein.pub/kidsfirst-login

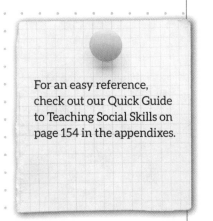
For an easy reference, check out our Quick Guide to Teaching Social Skills on page 154 in the appendixes.

identified. Let's say you are working on waiting for your turn; in this story you tell, you will want to embed self-talk ("I may want to go now, but I know I can wait"), strategies for success ("I will distract myself with a song"), and the eventual happy ending ("I waited my turn! That felt so good!"). Resources such as *The New Social Story Book* (2015) by Carol Gray and *The Social Skills Picture Book* (2001) by Jed Baker, can help you craft these stories in clear and powerful ways.

Role-playing will also involve the use of a story, but this time children will be the actors. You could set a few children up in the middle of the rug as the others watch in a circle. As you tell the story, they will act it out. When the time for a certain skill comes up, you might invite all the students to chime in and help the actors make the right choice.

Doing this once will have very little impact, but used repeatedly as a quick transitional activity—an end or a start to recess or choice time, or as a break between active times—can have a monumental impact on behavior.

Conclusion

When a child, or a group of children, enters our classrooms with significant needs in social-emotional learning, it can feel overwhelming and absolutely exhausting. As teachers, we can be quick to jump to passing the blame or seeing the situation as hopeless. But just as in reading or math or writing, we can start by getting to know our students, by being careful observers of their strengths and needs, and by finding something very small to build upon. This work can be slow and messy, but helping our students develop these social skills is one of the most important parts of our jobs as teachers.

Big Idea: Supporting Every Child

One Size Fits None: Tailoring Community Instruction to Each Kid

As teachers, we expect a range of learners to enter our classrooms. If a child comes to us at the beginning of the school year not meeting a reading benchmark, we wouldn't dream of labeling this child a "bad reader"—that would clearly be antithetical to our beliefs about growth and potential. Instead, we gather all the information we can about this child. We take running records, have conversations about books, assess high-frequency words, observe reading habits, and take stock of what strategies he knows and can use. And then we use all of that information to design tailored, thoughtful, and coherent reading instruction. We know it takes time. We know that small steps will be followed by big leaps followed by moments where it seems all has been forgotten, but we stick with it because we believe the ability to read can and will be learned. *Huge idea alert! Huge idea alert!* We can use the same process when it comes to behavior.

Let's dig in and talk about "that kid." The one who tests your boundaries. The one who keeps you up at night. The one people warned you about. Here is that huge idea one more time: "that kid" can and will learn how to be a productive and positive member of the community. She will learn ways of being in the world that will serve her well in the long run—as long as you're ready to help her, that is.

All too often children with deficits in social-emotional skills are quickly labeled *defiant*, *troubled*, *tricky*, *explosive*, or even *bad*. Kristi was one of these children. She spent a great deal of time sitting outside of her classroom in first grade, and second, and third, and so on, until one caring teacher taught her more productive ways of coping with her anger. (Thanks, Ms. Hannah!) Sometimes behaviors can seem so intense, so all encompassing, that our ability to see challenging behaviors as one small part of a child becomes impaired, and our view of the child can narrow to the point that all we can see are the "bad" behaviors. But just as with any academic area, we must take a step back and think as designers of learning. No matter how big, intrusive, infuriating, or explosive the behavior might be, we can figure something out. We can gather information, design instruction tailored to a student's needs, and get to work.

Adopt a Mantra, Change Your Mindset

If there is one mantra that you can keep in your head as you're trying to support a child with significant behavioral needs in your classroom (besides: *It's not about me, it's not about me*) we recommend this: *All behaviors are a form of communication.*

Ross Greene, a clinical psychologist and behavior specialist, writes, "Challenging behavior occurs when the demands and expectations being placed upon a child outstrip the skills he has to respond" (2008, 27). It's easy enough to imagine this in math. A child who is just learning addition might see an unfamiliar subtraction sign and add the numbers together. He just doesn't yet know how to do what is being asked of him. The same is true for a child who hits another child who interrupts her. Solving that problem with words may be as foreign to her as subtraction is to a child who is still working on mastering addition.

Greene suggests that we frame even the most challenging behaviors as lagging skills, and those times when they occur (during transitions, at points of frustration, when a child is hungry) as unsolved problems. When a child throws, swears, bolts, hits, or yells, she is trying to communicate that she does not yet have the skills to deal with the given situation. We've all been in deep water with our social skills from time to time; it is not a huge stretch of empathy to see how overwhelming the social expectations of school can be for certain children at certain times.

Let's oversimplify things for a moment and imagine that a child has an internal system like a car's engine. Most of the time things move along smoothly—you probably don't even notice your car's engine when you're doing errands or going on a road trip. But every once in awhile, when an engine gets overstressed, it starts to overheat, and an alarm sounds. If this happens, you don't just keep driving and hope for the best; you do something about it. You might add coolant, or turn off the AC, or pull over and wait for the engine to cool down. And eventually you'll need to find and fix the underlying reason the engine is overheating in the first place. Every time you see a child demonstrate a challenging behavior, what you're really seeing is a warning light, an attempt to communicate that his engine is overheating. Instead of adding more stress (asking a child to sit silently or engaging in a power struggle, for example), what we really need to do is figure out why the engine is overheating and what we can do about it.

After teaching for several years, it can feel easy to fall into the habit of saying, "I've had a child just like this before." In fact, it can be really helpful to look for patterns in behavior and development in children and to try out strategies that have worked for you in the past. But no two children are exactly alike. Be aware of the fact that although children are exhibiting similar behaviors, they might be doing it for entirely different reasons. To support every child in your class—especially those with the largest deficits in social-emotional skills—you will need to study their specific behaviors, make an individualized plan with tailored supports, and change and modify your instruction as the student gains new skills. Let's tackle this process step by step.

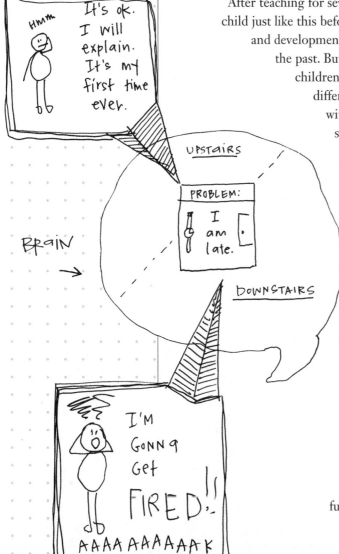

Upstairs Brains, Downstairs Brains, and the Science of Challenging Behaviors

Think about the last time you got really, really upset. So upset that maybe you said something and then instantly regretted the words that came out of your mouth. Maybe you were so mad that you could actually feel your face flush, your hands clench, and your heart start to beat faster. To better understand why we do some of those things (and why our students do, too), we need to take a closer look at what is actually happening in our brains.

Dr. Daniel Siegel, author of *The Whole Brain Child*, suggests that one way to understand the brain is to think of it as a house, with an upstairs and a downstairs (2011, 38).

The "upstairs" brain—the cerebral cortex—is sometimes called the "thinking" brain and is responsible for more sophisticated functions such as planning, problem solving, empathy, and inhibiting impulses. When you're planning your next math lesson or figuring out what to cook for dinner, you're using your upstairs brain. The "downstairs" brain—the amygdala, the brain stem, the limbic region—is responsible for housekeeping duties such as breathing and controlling body temperature, as well as controlling big emotions such as anger and fear. Most of the time you're not even aware of your downstairs brain, and usually these brain areas work seamlessly together. But stress, in many ways, acts like a locked door to the upstairs brain: the more stress we are placed under, the less access we have to that upstairs brain. There's actually a reason for the expression "you've flipped your lid." When we get really heated, really emotional, the upstairs part of our brain goes off line and the downstairs part of our brains takes over (Siegel 2011, 39–40). At that moment, our brains tell us to go into flight (storm out of a room), fight (yell, hit, kick), freeze (totally shut down), or flock (seek out the protection of others).

When a child's downstairs brain is controlling his actions, he is not intentionally choosing to yell at you or bolt out of the classroom. His actions are triggered by a sense of threat—and here the key is to reimagine the word *threat*—because the threat might just be that the child does not have the necessary social or emotional skills to handle the situation. A child with a low tolerance for distress might interpret "I don't know how to write the ideas I have" or "It's time to clean up and I'm not done" or "My friend is mad at me and likely to hate me forever" in a much different way than we would expect. The higher the state of the child's arousal (the hotter the engine, to return to the metaphor from before), the more she is reacting from her emotional brain rather than her logical brain.

In this moment, remember, unless you have a detached view of the behavior (as in "it's not about me" and "all behaviors are a form of communication" and not "this child hates me"), you have been placed under stress, too. You are likely not thinking with your upstairs brain, and your anger, frustration, or frozen response means your first response may not be the most helpful or productive one. Take a moment to recite those mantras, take a deep breath, and then address the situation.

Start from a Place of Genuine Curiosity

Observe behaviors and gather information. The first place you may want to start when addressing challenging behaviors is by *fixing everything right away*. We get it. That's why clip charts, sticker charts, and tally systems are so seductive: they are like hanging a picture to cover a crack in the wall. You may no longer see it, but as soon as you move the picture, the issue is there, possibly even worse than before. Same with challenging behaviors; if we remember that every behavior is a child trying to communicate lack of a skill he is compensating for, then it's much more helpful in the long run, for the benefit of the child's life in society, not just in our classroom, to determine what he's trying to communicate. Just as a child who is struggling with place value isn't going to necessarily say to you, "Gee, I could really use some help understanding the value of this digit," children struggling with behavior aren't going to say, "FYI, transition times are really tricky for me. I have a hard time going from one thing to another." We can start, then, by observing closely and asking ourselves and our colleagues questions.

How often do the challenging behaviors occur?

Are there specific times during the day or days of the week when you see the behavior?

If you notice that the behaviors happen more on Tuesday mornings or Thursday afternoons, can you determine if there's anything different about those days at school or at home?

Are the behaviors present more when certain children or adults are present?

Are there any fine/gross motor actions that seem to trigger the behavior?

In which places in the school (and classroom) does the behavior occur?

Do these behaviors occur more often during structured or unstructured times?

Are there any biological factors at play? Food? Sleep patterns?

What are you expecting the child to be doing when the behaviors occur?

DATA-GATHERING TIPS

Print out a copy of your weekly schedule and note exactly when and with whom (teachers, parents, and peers) the behavior occurs.

Sketch out a quick map of your classroom and note where in your space the behavior occurs.

Observe the child outside of the classroom setting. See what happens at recess, lunch, or art class.

Communicate regularly with the child's family and see if what you're noticing in school matches what they're noticing at home.

Develop a Plan

Once you sit down to answer some of those questions and really observe your student, you'll start to notice patterns and specific lagging skills. Maybe angry outbursts occur when there is a "zigzag" to the plan and the child has difficulty with flexibility. Perhaps a child has a hard time following directions when you just give them as spoken commands with no visuals. Or maybe a child hits another child when she feels left out or rejected. As in all aspects of teaching, pick a specific skill and a strategy to try first.

A quick note: the best time to start this conversation is not when you feel your own engine overheating. We are all human, we all have immediate reactions, we all react and overreact. Take a moment to breathe deeply, vent out your feelings of frustration privately, and then begin. You cannot help a child develop better community skills by forgoing your own modeling of behavior. We will have more to say about this in a minute.

Ross Greene (2008, 78) recommends three steps for solving these unsolved problems:

1. Empathize with the student.

2. Define adult concerns.

3. Offer an invitation.

This process might look familiar to those of you who confer and set goals with children. You start with research, state a teaching point, and then offer a strategy.

	PROCESS	ONE EXAMPLE OF WHAT THAT MIGHT SOUND LIKE	ANOTHER EXAMPLE OF WHAT THAT MIGHT SOUND LIKE
1. EMPATHIZE	For the first step, Greene suggests that we start the conversation by saying, "I've noticed that. . . . What's up?" He writes, "The goal of the empathy step is to achieve the best possible understanding of a kid's concern or perspective related to a given problem" (Greene 2008, 79). Of course, there will be many times where a child will not be able to tell you—or is not at all aware of—the why behind their behavioral challenges. In those cases, there's no reason to skip over the empathy step. There's no harm in asking and there's no harm in saying, "It can feel really hard. . . ."	**Teacher:** I've noticed that it's been hard for you to settle into math when lunch is over. What's up? **Child:** I don't like coming back to the classroom. **Teacher:** You don't like coming back to the classroom? Can you say more about that? **Child:** It's just so loud lining up after lunch and then we have to wait. **Teacher:** What do you mean? **Child:** I mean, everyone is loud in the cafeteria and then my energy gets all bubbled up and then math feels hard.	**Teacher:** So it seems that when it's time to clean up and you don't get to finish what you're writing, you get really upset. What's up? **Child:** It's just really annoying. I never get to finish. We always have to move on to science. **Teacher:** You get annoyed and feel like you never finish? Can you tell me more about that? **Child:** I have to stop in the middle of everything, I really hate stopping. The next day I can't remember what I was going to write.
2. DEFINE ADULT CONCERN	This is the step in the process where you identify the unsolved problem. Greene urges teachers to make sure this isn't a time to dwell on rules or even to focus on the solution to the problem. Instead, it should focus on how the problem is affecting the student or other people (Greene 2008, 90). It may feel hard to pull back or not sound judgmental in this step. This is a good time to remind yourself that at this moment your upstairs brain might be harder to access as well.	**Teacher:** I think I know what you're saying. The thing is, it's really important for your brain to be ready for math right when it starts. **Child:** I know. . . .	**Teacher:** I hear you. The tricky thing is that we all need to transition to science as a class. **Child:** Yeah.
3. INVITATION	The final step is where you work collaboratively to solve the problem. "The Invitation lets the kid know that solving the problem is something you're doing *with* him—in other words together—rather than to him" (Greene 2008, 92–93). At the end of this step, you'll have a realistic goal that works for both of you.	**Teacher:** I wonder if there's a way for us to solve this problem. I wonder how you could have lunch and then come back into the room ready to dive into math. Do you have any ideas? **Child:** Maybe I could eat lunch in the classroom? **Teacher:** Hmm. I usually have meetings during lunch and then I set up for math. But you could leave the lunchroom a little early and help me set up. Is that something you'd like to do? **Child:** Yeah, I'll try it.	**Teacher:** I think we can solve this problem. I wonder, how you could have a better idea about when the transition is happening? **Child:** I don't know. **Teacher:** Hmm. We have this timer that counts down and the red slides away. That way you would know when we're going to switch to science. Do you want to give that a try? **Child:** I guess.

Here Are Some Tools That Might Help

There are many different tools that you can use with children to help develop social skills. These tools scaffold the child's thinking and help to build habits and routines. However, like any good scaffolds, you should be thinking of how they can be removed. Our goal, even with a child with many challenging behaviors, is to help him become independent.

TOOL	HOW YOU MIGHT USE IT	EXAMPLE
Self-regulation options help children turn down their internal engines and help them develop an understanding of what a sense of calm feels like—an important piece of self-reflection.	As a class, create a list of options for self-regulation. Try to keep your list as broad as possible. Although some children benefit from deep breathing and sitting quietly, others need to move, rock, or lift heavy objects. Develop a system for accessing these breaks—maybe it's even a simple hand signal—and practice as a class.	
Problem scales, based on the work of Michelle Garcia Winner, Kari Dunn Buron, and The Autism Project of Illinois, help children identify the "size" of the problem and possible solutions.	Teach and create a problem scale with your whole class. Then, as small and big problems arise, use it as a tool to reflect on and solve the problems themselves. Make sure you teach into strategies for solving each size problem. Bummer: Get a paper towel to wipe up a spill. Problem: Rock, paper, scissors to see who uses the book first. Disaster: Get a teacher's attention when a mouse scurries across the floor.	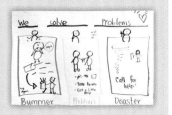
Self-talk is comprised of mantras or directions we give ourselves to navigate tricky emotional situations.	Work with children to develop mantras or phrases they find soothing or helpful. Maybe a child who feels like he never gets a chance could say, "Everyone needs a turn; I will get mine soon."	
Social stories are highly visual books about a specific situation, social concept, or skill. They help children understand what to expect in a certain situation and what is expected of them. Developed by Carol Gray (2015) and Jed Baker (2001), these books capitalize on the power of narrative to shape behavior.	Social stories can be cowritten by a whole class, by a small group, or one-on-one. You can use photographs and make it as specific to the situation and the skill as possible. In the previous example, the teacher might create a social story for the child about coming back to the classroom early to set up for math.	
Personal visual schedules and supports can help in the same way that they do with a whole class. Personal visual supports can be created to target the specific skill you are working on with a child, from how to get organized for reading workshop to what to do when you're really mad.	As teachers, we have a tendency to be very verbal. When you're trying to support a student's behavioral challenges, the last thing you want to do is talk, talk, talk at the child. Instead, rely on visual supports to do the communicating. You can also get into the habit of making visual supports on the fly. A quick sketch can really support a child, especially when she's in the downstairs brain. If you make them small and easily accessible, these supports can be tucked away during times of the day when they're not needed.	

Real Talk: Sometimes It Gets Really, Really Hard

This is one of those times in our book when we want you, dear reader, to know we have been in your shoes. We have been brought to tears in the bathroom by challenging behaviors, and we have worked with children day in and day out to help them learn self-regulation, to make friends, to solve problems. There are few things more exhausting—physically and emotionally—than having a child or a number of children in our classrooms with intensive behavioral challenges. We know in our bones how hard it can be to come to school day after day not knowing what the day will bring. We know what it takes to teach and nurture a child who spends most of her life in her downstairs brain. We know what it feels like to keep your head level when all you want to do is to run out of the school and eat a pound of chocolate. As challenging as these moments are, it's our job to be problem solvers.

There are a series of steps you can take to de-escalate really hard moments, and we'll get to those in a moment, but the first step is to make sure you are calm enough and in control enough to handle the situation.

Ross Greene writes, "Separation of affect refers to the ability to separate the emotions (affect) you're feeling in response to a problem or frustration from the thinking you must do to resolve the problem" (Greene 2008, 20). The more in control we can stay as teachers, the better problem solvers we can be. It can be hard to admit it, but heightened behaviors are often co-constructed. Big affect—big emotions—are contagious.

Researcher Stephen Porges found that people "unconsciously send signals we unconsciously receive and process. When the person is attuned and non-judgmental, their signals give us a sense of physical and emotional safety. When we feel our guard letting down, the vagus nerve is slowing our heart rate and activating our calming parasympathetic nervous system. If we are with a calming person when the amygdala fires off, their presences overrides the effect of the stress hormones, and calms us" (in Bunn 2016).

When it comes to de-escalating especially tricky moments, it's helpful to have a go-to set of steps to turn to. Before we can problem solve, we need to help the child regain self-control. Mark Goulston, author of *Just Listen*, notes that in these moments it's really important to keep the focus not on you, as in "I know you want to follow my directions," but on their own self-interest, experiences, and feelings (2009, 208). To do so, we help children reconnect their upstairs brain to their downstairs brain; we help them notice what's happening in their bodies; and we stay by their side, even when doing so is very, very hard. The following steps can help you guide your student through this process:

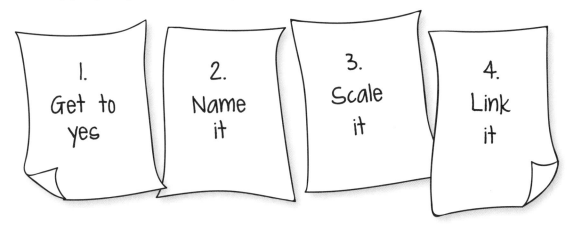

1. Get to yes

2. Name it

3. Scale it

4. Link it

	WHAT IT IS	WHAT IT MIGHT SOUND LIKE
1. **GET TO YES**	When a child is operating solely in his downstairs (think fight-or-flight) brain, our first step is to get him to start using his upstairs, or logical, brain. These questions are like "contact statements" to help you reconnect areas of the brain. Ask a series of questions that get him to say (or yell), "Yes" (Goulston 2009, 206).	In this scenario, a first grader yells and tips over chairs after hearing that the class will be having indoor recess. The child hides under the easel, kicking the wall, and refuses to get out. T: Are you really, really mad right now? S: Yes! T: Are you really mad at me right now? S: Yes!
2. **NAME IT**	Next, name the problem in simple, nonjudgmental terms. This should be another opportunity to get him to say, "Yes."	T: You're really angry because we can't go outside today. S: Yes!
3. **SCALE IT**	Help the child identify where in his body he's feeling the strong emotion or ask him to scale it from small to big with his hands. Even if the problem seems very small to you, the reflective work of thinking through the problem is what's reactivating the child's upstairs brain.	T: Where in your body do you feel the mad? S: [points to chest] T: Are you a little mad, or a lot mad? Can you show me with your hands? S: [holds hands far apart]
4. **LINK IT**	Your main goal now is to develop a plan that enables the child to regulate, stay safe, and rejoin the group. This might mean taking a break away in a quiet corner of a classroom or going for a walk. Rocking, rhythms, bouncing a ball, or doing something repetitive in nature can help a child regulate, too. When the child has regulated (which might take quite some time or might not even be until the next day), you can help guide him through a reflective process to think about how he might have solved the problem in a different way. This is another great opportunity for role-playing and practice.	T: The reason you're so angry is because we can't go outside today. It's raining so the plan changed. S: I hate indoor recess. It's so boring. T: I know you're still upset, but are you ready to solve this problem with me? S: I guess so. T: Let's go for a quick walk and figure out what you'd like to do for indoor recess.* Alternate ending: S: No. T: OK, why don't you head to the beanbag, set the timer, and come and get me when you feel ready to make a plan. S: OK. (If the child does not come to get you when the timer goes off, check back in.)

*We *promise* we know that not all escalations are solved so easily. And we know that it's hard to keep this all in mind when you're in one of *those* moments. But we also know that tackling these moments from a place of empathy and problem solving is the best way for you and for your students.

Conclusion: Rome Wasn't Built in a Day; Kids Won't Learn Everything About Your Community Overnight

When we talk to new and experienced teachers alike, one of the main comments we hear is that they felt unprepared for some of the realities of the classroom. You may have on-the-job training about teaching reading or math, but it is rare to learn more about how to build better communities. Often, we are all just doing the best we can without a lot of guidance, but there is information out there to help us do better. The books we've mentioned and the resources we've cited should be your next stop. The classrooms we build will help children form expectations and hopes for the world at large; it is our ethical and social responsibility to move past "good enough" when it comes to social skills and community building.

We teach children how to read, how to solve complex math problems, and how to write essays. We also teach children how to be the best people they can be, so we can help them create the best world possible. And now that we all know better, we can do better each day in our communities.

Moofus and Mallant Talk Teaching

Highlights magazine, the iconic institution that it is, taught many of us about proper behavior through two brothers named Goofus and Gallant. In every issue Goofus would do something terrible, like push a baby off a swing, and Gallant would demonstrate the more socially acceptable option of waiting to take turns on the swing, like saying "Can I go next?" There are many Goofus and Gallant learning opportunities in teaching, but because they are copyrighted characters, we'd like to introduce you to our two teaching sisters: Moofus, the sister most likely to lead you to an early retirement, and Mallant, our heroine and mentor in all things challenging. So let's say our sisters are facing a tough day in the classroom. What will they do?

What Is Happening	Moofus Says	Mallant Says (and Is Backed by Research and Common Sense)
The class is becoming rowdy.	Start yelling and don't stop! Be the loudest one in the room! Bring up every time your class has ignored you! Vent your demons! Try yelling, "You never listen!"	Take a deep breath, talk quietly, or even sing your next direction to get the class' attention. The change in volume often attracts more attention. (More in "Build a Community, Don't Just Manage One")
The child states he or she is upset about something that seems minor.	Deny those feelings! You can't be sad over small things! Those are the rules! Say, "Don't be ridiculous!"	Restate. Try saying "I hear you" as in "I hear that you are really angry because your granola bar has raisins in it." This is more likely to calm the child and lead to resolution. (More in "Supporting Every Child")
You are caught in a power struggle with a student.	Never give up! Your parents didn't raise a quitter! You will win this battle even if you can never leave this location.	It's OK to walk away. Try saying, "It sounds like we both need a minute. I will come back to talk to you again. I want to help us come to a solution." Side note: If this is during an emergency, like a fire, don't give them a minute, get them out the door to safety. (More in "Supporting Every Child")

Allyson Black-Foley is a licensed psychotherapist serving nearly 500 young people as the Head of Counseling Services at a school in Philadelphia. Allyson has implemented programs to address the traumas of incarceration, community violence, and structural racism through partnerships with local organizations. We asked her about what classroom teachers need to know about trauma and how they can support students who have experienced trauma in their classrooms.

Q How does trauma affect children? What behaviors might a teacher notice?

A Trauma affects children in myriad ways, and can look very different depending on the child. Trauma impacts a child's ability to manage their feelings and behavior, learn and retain information, and build relationships (Rossen and Hull 2012). Children who experienced trauma during their preverbal stage will not have the language to express what happened to them. Lacking the words to express their experiences, these children may express their pain by becoming oppositional or destructive (Cole et al. 2005). While these behaviors can look like acting out behaviors, they may point to a trauma background, especially in cases of sudden onset (NCTSNSC 2008). In addition to becoming oppositional or destructive, students may also exhibit hypervigilance, avoidance, reactive responses in the face of minor disappointments, or have difficulty staying on task (Cole et al. 2005).

Q What are some things teachers can do in their classrooms to support a child who has experienced trauma?

A Traditional methods of addressing negative classroom behaviors are not suitable or effective for students impacted by trauma. Students who have experienced trauma often need modifications and extra supports to be successful in school. Just as students with learning differences need accommodations, so do students impacted by trauma.

Compared to their counterparts, students who have experienced trauma may have more difficulty with self-regulation and self-soothing (Cole et al. 2005). "Traumatic experiences can disrupt the ability of children to learn and process verbal information and use language as a vehicle for communication. These language problems can undermine literacy skills, social-emotional development, and behavioral self-regulation" (Cole et al. 2005, 22). In keeping with this understanding of trauma's impact, it is important for teachers to respond to challenging behaviors using quiet tones, avoiding power battles, and focusing on de-escalation before responding with disciplinary procedures. These techniques can help students gain a sense of control while building their emotional regulation skills.

Some basic tenets of trauma-informed practice teachers can incorporate in their work with students include:

- ⭐ Frame your thinking in terms of "what has this student experienced?" instead of "what's wrong with this student?"

- ⭐ In the face of escalation, respond with statements such as "I see you," "I'm here with you," and "I hear you." This can be very calming for traumatized students.

- ⭐ Offer choices. This is especially important for those who feel out of control in other aspects of their lives.

- ⭐ Provide regular movement breaks, which has been shown to lead to better attention and learning (Fecser 2015).

"Just as students with learning differences need accommodations, so do students impacted by trauma."

Here are some other resources you can turn to for more information:

- ❤ *Supporting and Educating Traumatized Students: A Guide for School-Based Professionals* edited by Eric Rossen and Robert Hull (2012)

- ❤ *The Body Keeps the Score: Brain, Mind, and Body in the Healing of Trauma* by Bessel van der Kolk (2015)

- ❤ *Helping Traumatized Children Learn: Supportive School Environments for Children Traumatized by Family Violence* by Susan Cole et al. (2005)

- ❤ *Trauma Stewardship: An Everyday Guide to Caring for Self While Caring for Others* by Laura van Dernoot Lipsky and Connie Burk (2009)

- ❤ *Lost at School: Why Our Kids with Behavioral Challenges are Falling Through the Cracks and How We Can Help Them* by Ross W. Greene (2008)

Another effective way to work with students who have experienced trauma is to prioritize the teacher-student relationship. Students respond better to adults with whom they have a strong rapport. Research has shown that if a student has a positive relationship with a teacher, they show fewer aggressive behaviors in the classroom (Baker, Grant, and Morlock 2008). "…Teachers may act as compensatory resources for these vulnerable children, helping them to navigate the social world of school and providing the emotional security necessary for learning and school adaptation" (5).

Teachers can also play a vital role in advocating for interventions that address the underlying issues, rather than behavioral modifications that only address symptoms for those with possible trauma histories. To determine what attribution to make for the child's behaviors, teachers can encourage a formal evaluation by a mental health professional. Early intervention is key, as untreated childhood trauma can have lasting adverse outcomes into adulthood (Rahim, 2014; Shonkoff and Garner 2012; Plumb, Bush, and Kersevich 2016).

It is a daunting task for teachers to manage the emotional reactions of students impacted by trauma while managing a classroom. However, utilizing tenets of trauma-informed practice can help teachers understand and support their students in a new way, leading to better educational outcomes for those impacted by trauma.

Q What do you wish all teachers knew about teaching children who have experienced trauma?

A The most important thing for teachers to know is that helping students impacted by trauma begins with self-reflection and awareness. A student may act in ways that make their teacher feel the same way they feel, trigging their teacher's stress response (Cole et al. 2005). As a result, teachers can begin to feel helpless, out of control, angry, or agitated. There are skills teachers can learn to manage their emotional reactions so they can model the self-regulation expected of students.

Effective de-escalation hinges on the teacher's ability to recognize their own emotions and triggers. The practice of becoming mindful in moments of escalation can help teachers see situations clearly, respond calmly, and skillfully de-escalate students. This approach has a dual benefit: the student de-escalates and the teacher-student relationship is strengthened, a key ingredient to success in school (Dods 2013).

It is important to remember that students who have experienced trauma are incredibly resilient. Teachers can have a significant impact on these students' lives by using trauma-informed practice in the classroom, affirming children's feelings and experiences, and speaking to children's resiliency.

4

Building Curriculum

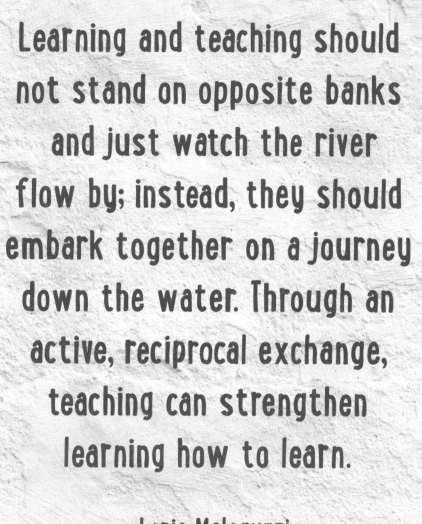

Learning and teaching should not stand on opposite banks and just watch the river flow by; instead, they should embark together on a journey down the water. Through an active, reciprocal exchange, teaching can strengthen learning how to learn.

—Loris Malaguzzi,
"History, Ideas, and Basic Philosophy"

Introduction

If we believe that children are, by their very nature, competent, creative, empathetic, and curious, then our curriculum must reflect those beliefs. Every instructional move we make as teachers sends a message. When we just tell our students that four times four is sixteen, four times five is twenty, and then hand them a worksheet to practice, we're sending the message that the world of math is just a world of memorization, not a complex and deeply interconnected system.

Alternatively, how powerful is it when children discover, through playing, building, noticing, experimenting, that multiples of four have a unique connection, a connection they can deeply understand and represent as (eureka!) four times four?! In this latter example, we send the message that knowledge isn't something we (the mighty and powerful teachers) disseminate, but rather something that the students construct and something that we nurture and cultivate and watch, like a tender green shoot unfurling from the soil for the first time. How lucky are we, as teachers, to witness the magic and the mystery of neurons firing and children learning?

Patience, faith, and the ability to truly *see* what children are showing us is the cornerstone of responsive teaching. Orchestrating the growth of all of one's students across several content areas is a daunting task for even the most veteran teachers. This section will provide you with strategies to help answer the question: what do my children need to be successful and happy? Answering this question will help you keep moving children toward curriculum goals in the most powerful way possible—by seeing exactly what children are doing and by teaching exactly what they need next.

We ground this work in three big ideas:

The first big idea, *curriculum should be responsive and intentional*, makes the case that teachers can and should balance curriculum-driven and kid-driven instruction. We offer tips for studying the children in your class and balancing their needs with what you're "supposed to" teach.

The next big idea, *build a better teaching toolbox: clear teaching structures drive complex learning*, lays out tried-and-true teaching structures from workshop model to one-on-one conferring. These structures will form the foundation for your teaching and a springboard for your innovation.

The final big idea, *responsive teachers draw from all they know*, helps teachers think about how elements such as time, level of preference, group size, and degree of familiarity affect learning. We will take a look at a writing workshop and see how one teacher's small adjustments can lead to big impacts on engagement and learning.

You'll notice that this section doesn't necessarily tell you *what* to teach—we know that most likely you have a long list of standards and a districtwide curriculum that takes care of that; instead, we give suggestions on *how* to teach, regardless of the curriculum in place. And, just in case your interest is piqued, we've tucked in many of our favorite resources on both content and teaching practices so you'll have plenty of experts to turn to as you dive deeper into teaching and learning. These suggestions aim to steer any curriculum toward a more student-focused classroom—helping us walk the walk, not just talk the talk when it comes to putting our beliefs into practice.

Big Idea: Curriculum Should Be Responsive and Intentional

Every August Christine has a recurring first-day-of-school dream. It starts off idyllically: the sun is shining, the birds are chirping, the buses pull up, her students enter smiling. Then, as the dark storm clouds roll in, she looks down at their faces and starts to sweat. Her dream always ends with the same terror-filled question: *But what am I supposed to teach them?!* Kristi's August back-to-school dream involves the kids arriving before her and the classroom in utter chaos—she thought she had one more day! She doesn't even know where to start. For some teachers, the non–dream world answer is a straightforward—whatever the curriculum says next—and for others, it's wherever the children lead us today. We believe it's possible to find a happy medium where your curriculum is guided by the real needs of your students and by the intentional, responsive choices you make as a teacher. But before we delve into how to make this happen (and how to avoid the August night sweats), let's take a closer look at the difference between curriculum-driven and kid-driven instruction.

Curriculum-Driven Instruction

In the most extreme sense of this concept, a teacher driven by curriculum knows what he is teaching on day 172 of school when it's only day thirty. Sometimes this comes in the form of scripted programs, programs that tell you on day fourteen you have to say these exact words in this exact order for children to learn how to infer character feelings. Less extreme examples would be when schools and teachers plan for children to achieve an end product with very specific indicators, for example, a math problem must be solved with a specific algorithm. You are likely more driven by curriculum if your plan book is written in for weeks ahead of time, and you have even longer-term highly specific plans saved somewhere.

The idea behind curriculum-driven instruction is that children need to acquire certain pieces of knowledge, in a specific order, during a specific grade, to learn all they need to learn. More often than not, when this is the dominant mode of thought, teachers feel comfortable doing the same thing year after year because the knowledge children need to acquire is the same year after year. Likewise, schools that believe strongly in this concept might even require teachers across a grade to be teaching the same things on the same days.

The challenge with depending solely on curriculum is that this method fails to take into account children's own unique development, interests, and passions. This method relies on expecting every child to achieve the same goals in the same way, even if other ways (and other goals) would be better for some children. This can lead to a certain degree of passivity for children in their learning lives, because their role within the system is simply to receive knowledge.

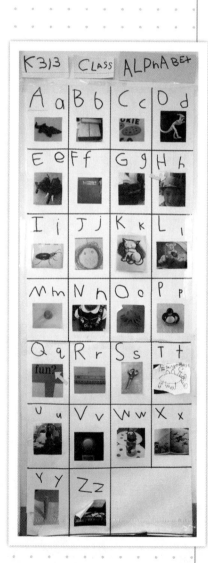

Kid-Driven Instruction

In the most extreme sense of this concept, there is no way a teacher could tell you what she is doing on day thirty if it is day four. A teacher driven by this style of instruction is likely to spend more time reflecting on observations and children's actions and questions than on planning ahead. Teachers are using what they notice one day to inform what they will do, ask, or introduce the following day. This is often described as "emergent curriculum" or "responsive curriculum" because it emerges from the students' interests, and we respond to their actions and choices. Reggio Emilia educators have been constructing their curriculum in this way for decades and, more recently, the project-based learning model aims to do the same. In both of these cases, children have more autonomy over what they are learning and their interests drive how the teacher plans to support their growth and development.

The theory behind kid-driven instruction is that children construct knowledge through experiences and through reflecting on those experiences. What better way to help children construct their knowledge of the world than by letting their wonderings, questions, and creations guide a curriculum? In this case, a curriculum emerges from the work children are doing; no two classrooms of the same grade would be doing the exact same work, and no year would look the same because the children, their passions, and their ways of learning would all be different.

The challenge of building curriculum from the ground up with kids is that it can be easy to get stumped with where to go next and it can be hard to ensure that every child is having access to similar information. It can be hard to keep track of and ensure that all of the "have-tos," such as the Common Core Standards or district requirements, are met. This style of teaching requires ample time for reflection and conversation between colleagues and can feel scary and unwieldy to new teachers, or teachers without a firm grounding in child development as well as literacy and math development.

Finding the Sweet Spot Right in the Middle

The reality of our educational system is that we are not all in schools that have the resources, time, or the capability to move to a fully kid-driven curriculum. Many of us have curricula handed to us, and full days are spent planning out a whole month's or year's worth of teaching. However, just because this is our starting point does not mean it should be our ending point. Children deserve to be active participants in their education and crafters of their own learning paths. When we encourage this, we encourage active, powerful thinkers rather than passive receptors of knowledge. Even if a curriculum is handed to us, it is our responsibility to be responsive to the children we are teaching. The results of lesson one will invariably alter the course and trajectory of lesson two, which will have impacts on the way lesson three is taught or perhaps even skipped.

We do not believe that any instruction should be scripted and mandated because it removes the relationship between teacher and child. That does not mean you have to light your school's curriculum on fire, but it does mean getting smarter about how to assess what children love and need to learn and how to adjust our teaching to better respond to that.

For more on motivation and engagement read:

- ❤ *Drive: The Surprising Truth About What Motivates Us* by Daniel Pink (2011)
- ❤ *Mindset: The New Psychology of Success* by Carol Dweck (2008)
- ❤ *A Mindset for Learning: Teaching the Traits of Joyful, Independent Growth* by Kristi and Christine (2015)

CHECK YOURSELF—WHERE IS YOUR TEACHING COMING FROM?

We have found it very helpful to create a set of reflective questions you can ask yourself when you're deciding if and how to teach something. Here are a few of our favorites that we use often:

→ **If a child asks, "Why are we doing this?" do I know why?** We try to ground our teaching in authentic practice. As much as possible, our lessons and units are planned around the "real" work of writers, readers, scientists, and mathematicians. We want our students to be building the habits of thinkers, problem solvers, and change agents ready to affect their own community and the world.

→ **Will the final product look the same?** If so, how can I provide more opportunities for creativity and personalization? Our whole class can write stories, but the stories don't all need to be about our field trip to the fire station or what we did over summer vacation. When we start teaching something, we try to see all of the possible ways that children can have choice and autonomy in their work.

→ **Will all students be able to access this and will they all be able to see that they're improving?** Educational theorist Lev Vygotsky (1978) holds that children make their best growth when they are working in their zones of proximal development (the place between what they can do independently and what they need support to do). All learners—adults and children alike—do better when they are learning from a place where they feel capable and empowered. For more on helping all children access their learning, and specifically children on individualized education plans, see our interview with Special Educator Annie Dunn on page 139.

→ **Is there a sense of joy?** Loris Malaguzzi, one of the founders of the Reggio Emilia schools, has a quote about teaching and learning that simply says, "Nothing without joy." We ask ourselves, as often as possible, is what we are doing instilling a sense of wonder, creativity, and playfulness? Is there a buzz of excitement when it's time for book clubs and a groan when writing is done? No matter what we're teaching, we try to keep joy and curiosity at its heart.

We often field questions from teachers about how to motivate students, how to keep children of all ages engaged, and how to increase stamina. Like many educators, we believe that stamina and motivation are both products of engagement. As teachers, it's our responsibility to reflect on exactly what it is we are asking children to be motivated about and engaged in. When we do this, we find that the more our teaching can stay true to our beliefs about children and learning, the more intrinsically engaged our students are.

Responsive Means Ask First, Teach Later

In many classrooms across the country, teachers are handed a math, reading, writing, spelling, science, or social studies curriculum that is neatly laid out with just enough sessions to get them through the year. Many come in shiny binders with satisfying organizational tabs and easy-to-copy resources in the back. On one hand, you might think, "Phew! At least one thing's off my plate." And trust us, we've been there. But on the other hand, we've also been in the position of teaching an entire preprescribed unit only to realize that (a) the majority of the children could meet the objectives before the unit even began or (b) very few of the children could come close to meeting the objectives after the unit wrapped up. *Embarrassing teaching moments alert!* Early in her teaching career, Christine was a week into a first-grade unit on three-dimensional shapes, only to realize that many of her students had no idea what the difference was between a rhombus and a trapezoid. Meanwhile, Kristi was set to launch a unit on how-to writing when a second grader interrupted to ask if she was referring to "procedural texts."

So what do we do? As teachers, we need to pause before launching into something new and figure out exactly what our students know and what they need to learn. So, please, give yourself permission to put the binder back on the shelf for just a moment and take some very valuable time to study your students.

Studying Kids

When you are studying your children to make your teaching more responsive, remember to keep the emphasis on what they can do, not on what you've already taught. Even if it's mid-March and you've taught two units on informational writing, you'll need to see what really stuck, not just what you feel like you've already covered.

It can be tempting to limit our observations to just the content we're trying to cover. But if we're trying to teach the whole child, it's important to study many aspects of their learning.

LENSES TO LOOK THROUGH

WHAT TO STUDY	WHAT TO LOOK FOR
CONTENT	What skills and strategies are they using? What are they "using but confusing"? What can they tell you about a given topic, skill, or strategy?
ENGAGEMENT	What is their level of interest? Are they buzzing over the content, rushing to get started, or staring aimlessly and looking for reasons to linger around the garbage can? Are they able to sustain focus for the whole time? What questions or wonderings are they bringing up?
CHOICE	What topics are they writing about? What books do they gravitate toward? What are they doing in their free time?
MINDSET	What is the children's self-view in this area? Confident? A bit hesitant? Wary of mistakes? What do they do when they come to a challenge?
COMMUNITY	How are students working together? How are they using empathy, critical thinking, and compromise? What's the feeling of the community during this time? Is there a buzz around the learning?
INDEPENDENCE	What are students doing on their own? What scaffolds do they rely on?

For more on helping children develop their own self-identities and the class' inclusivity, see our interview with Sara Ahmed on page 27 of Section 1.

With these guiding questions in mind . . .

. . . we start to gather information on our students.

GATHERING INFORMATION	
METHOD	**WHAT YOU DO**
OBSERVATIONS	Take time to sit back and observe what the students in your class do during a specific time. Jennifer Serravallo (2010) suggests watching a workshop and noting how often students' eyes are on their books, how often they're looking out the window, and how often they're glancing up at you. You might also choose to observe one specific student at different times over the course of a few days to get an even deeper understanding of him as a learner.
INTERVIEWS	Ask your students a set of questions—either by writing or by conversation—to see what they know about a certain topic or skill. Some teachers (especially of older students) have used Google Forms to gather information, from book preferences to background knowledge to a student's identity as a mathematician.
WORK SAMPLES AND PHOTOGRAPHS	Work samples cover a wide range of both work for assessment purposes and work that happens daily. Some possibilities include: • Student writing: on-demand, or day-to-day work. (See Carl Anderson's *Assessing Writers* [2015], Jennifer Serravallo's *Writing Strategies Book: Your Everything Guide to Developing Skilled Writers* [2017], or *Writing Pathways: Performance Assessments and Learning Progressions* [Calkins 2014] for more information.) • Running records, reading logs, Post-its, and student talk around books. (See Marie Clay's *Running Records for Classroom Teachers* [2017], Jennifer Serravallo's *The Reading Strategies Book: Your Everything Guide to Developing Skilled Readers* [2015], Fountas and Pinnell's *Guided Reading: Responsive Teaching Across the Grades* [2016], and Stephanie Harvey and Anne Goudvis' *Strategies That Work: Teaching Comprehension for Understanding, Engagement, and Building Knowledge* [2017] for more.) • Math work, exit tickets, math interviews, and investigations. (See the Math in Practice series by Sue O'Connell et al. [2016] for more.) Lucky for us, it's getting easier and easier to curate these work samples with our phones and apps, such as Seesaw and Evernote, that help to store and organize digital collections and photographs. (For more on digital curation, see Katie Muhtaris and Kristin Ziemke's *Amplify: Digital Teaching and Learning in the K–6 Classroom* [2015].)
VIDEOS	For a long time, teachers have relied on audio transcripts and videos to help them capture important moments in the classroom. With the advent of smart phones and tablets it is easier than ever. You might find it helpful to record a whole-class conversation or an inquiry group and watch to note the intricacies of the conversation that might have escaped you in the moment.

Making and Using a Checklist

One of the most important things for you to keep in mind when it comes to using a checklist is that it's an opportunity for you to look honestly at what your students have learned, not what you have taught—which might be two different things. Anyone who thought they taught an elaboration strategy in writing only to find the skill absent from everyone's work the day after the lesson knows the truth of that. The key to being responsive is to be realistic and comfortable with what your students know. Some students will be way behind what they're *supposed to* know, and others will be way beyond what the curricular tools suggest you teach them next.

We're going to guide you step-by-step through the process of using a checklist to study what your students know and then plan for your responsive instruction.

Step 1:

Determine what you'd like your students to know by the end of your next unit.

You might base this information on:

- what the majority of your students already know and what the "next steps" could be

- the Common Core State Standards and your district's or school's expectations for your students

- bigger goals for your class such as collaborating or using self-talk for problem solving

- other guiding questions from the table on page 112.

Tip: Make a copy of your checklist *now* to use at the end of your unit to assess your students' learning.

K – Independent Writing Projects

	Many words	stretching	speech bubbles	small action	detailed pics	multiple pages	one idea					
Anna												
Arjun												
Benji												
Ernie												
Grace												
Harry												
Jack												
Jaxson												
Jordan												
Kevin												
Lettie												
Lexie												
Malini												
Max												
Micah												
Mila												
Mira												
Phillippe												
Princess												
Ray												
Sidney												

Step 2:

Look closely at student work and fill in your checklist.

This student work could include work samples, interviews, observations, or any other means of gathering data. If you're not sure about a student's performance on a given item, seek more information.

Tip: By using a plus-or-minus system, a minus can easily turn into plus as you begin to teach the unit or if you've incorrectly assessed a student (it happens!).

K – Independent Writing Projects

	Many words	stretching	speech bubbles	small action	detailed pics	multiple pages	one idea						
Anna	+	+	–	+	–	+	+						
Arjun	–	–	–	–	+	+	+						
Benji	+	+	–	–	+	+							
Ernie	+	+	–	–	+	–	+						
Grace	+	+	+	+	+	+	+						
Harry	+	+	—	–	+	+	+						
Jack	–	–	–	–	+	+	+						
Jaxson	+	+	—	–	+	+	+						
Jordan	+	+	–	–	+	+							
Kevin	+	+	–	+	+	+	–						
Lettie	+	–	–	–	+	+	+						
Lexie	+	+	–	–	–	+	+						
Malini	+	+	+	+	+	–	+						
Max	+	–	–	–	–	+	+						
Micah	–	–	–	–	+	+	+						
Mila	+	+	–	+	+	+	+						
Mira	?	+	–	–	+	+	+						
Phillippe	+	+	–	–	+	+	+						
Princess	+	+	–	–	–	+	+						
Ray	+	+	–	+	+	+	–						
Sidney	+	+	–	–	+	+	+						

Step 3:

Highlight what students need to work on and look for patterns.

Take out your highlighters and channel your love for color coding and get to work! Start by highlighting what students need to work on and start to notice patterns.

Tip: You'll get a different picture of your class if you highlight by goal rather than by student.

K – Independent Writing Projects

	Many words	stretching	speech bubbles	small action	detailed pics	multiple pages	one idea						
Anna	+	+	–	+	–	+	+						
Arjun	–	–	–	–	+	+	+						
Benji	+	+	—	–	+	+							
Ernie	+	+	–	–	+	–	+						
Grace	+	+	+	+	+	+	+						
Harry	+	+	—	–	+	+	+						
Jack	–	–	•	–	+	+	+						
Jaxson	+	+	—	–	+	+	+						
Jordan	+	+	—	–	–	+	+						
Kevin	+	+	—	+	+	+	–						
Lettie	+	–	—	–	+	+	+						
Lexie	+	+	–	—	+	+							
Malini	+	+	+	+	+	–	+						
Max	+	–	–	—	+	+							
Micah	–	–	–	–	+	+	+						
Mila	+	+	–	+	+	+	+						
Mira	?	+	—	–	+	+	+						
Phillippe	+	+	—	–	+	+	+						
Princess	+	+	–	–	+								
Ray	+	+	–	+	+	+	–						
Sidney	+	+	—	–	+	+	+						

For more on observing students read:

- ♥ *The Art of Classroom Inquiry: A Handbook for Teacher-Researchers* by Ruth Shagoury Hubbard and Brenda Miller Power (2003)
- ♥ *Reflecting Children's Lives: A Handbook for Planning Your Child-Centered Curriculum* by Deb Curtis and Margie Carter (2011)

Step 4:

Choose the big goals you'll be working on with the whole class during the unit.

What are four big goals that most of your students need? These goals will be the driving focus of your unit.

Now's the time to take out your curriculum tools and see what you can use for resources. You might take your math unit and flip through the lessons and decide which to skip and which to teach. If your students need it, go back to an earlier unit or even another grade level and use the lessons or ideas that best fit their needs.

Take out four blank pieces of paper and write one goal at the top of each piece of paper. Then, come up with four or five focus lessons for each goal. These focus lessons will become your whole-class lessons.

Tip: Design the anchor chart that will complement your goals and reflect the language you'll use with students right on these planning pages and *voilà!* that's ready to go now, too. For more on anchor charts see *Smarter Charts, K-2: Optimizing an Instructional Staple to Create Independent Readers and Writers* (2012) and *Smarter Charts for Math, Science, and Social Studies: Making Learning Visible in the Content Areas* (2014) by our very own Kristi Mraz and her coauthor Marjorie Martinelli.

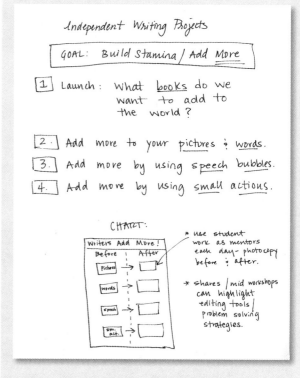

Step 5:

Plan for small groups and individual conferences.

Chances are some students will need to work on *all* of the objectives you've included on your checklist and others won't need to work on any of them. The checklist can be your starting point for small groups and one-on-one conferences.

Tip: Transfer the next steps from your checklist right onto your small-group planning templates and conferring notes. You can find samples of all of these templates in the appendixes.

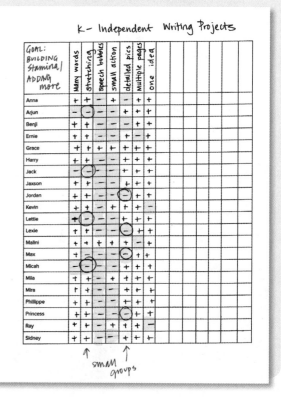

Ready, Set, Teach! And Reteach!

When all of your instruction, investigating, risk taking, and the messy work of learning is wrapped up for this unit, you'll want to return to your checklist and gather new work samples. In an old-school version of teaching, you might teach something once, assess it in a whole-class manner, and then move on. It may have been an easier world to teach in, but chances are, a whole lot of kids were missing a whole lot of learning. Now, we are constantly in a cycle of teaching, assessing, modifying, and teaching again. Remember to keep focused on what the students have actually learned—what elements of your teaching really stuck. For example, even though you *know* that Sara was in a small group on building arrays to solve multiplication problems, there's nothing to gain from dragging her to that goal if she needs to work her way up to it, and, as a responsive teacher, you'll make sure that there are other opportunities for Sara to learn that strategy.

Setting goals for your instruction is just the first step to being a truly responsive teaching. In the next section, we offer many different structures for *how* you might teach and the rationale for picking each one.

Big Idea: Build a Better Teaching Toolbox: Clear Teaching Structures Drive Complex Learning

Think back to those days when you first started to cook. Chances are, if you're like us, you relied heavily on recipes. When Kristi first started making chili, she would follow the recipe to the letter. But now that she understands the basic ratios, she'll add a little of this and a little of that, depending on what needs to be cleaned out of the fridge. That's the thing—once you get to know and practice your basic recipes enough, you can be more creative and daring. The teaching structures we're about to lay out for you can be thought of as your basic recipes. In teaching, as in cooking, once you start to see how basic components work together and how different teaching structures work, you can set aside your cookbook and innovate. It's in this innovation and experimentation that you find your real responsiveness as a teacher.

In this section we will outline the basic elements of each of these teaching structures:

- ⭐ workshop models
- ⭐ focus lessons
- ⭐ small groups
- ⭐ conferring
- ⭐ reflective conversations.

Masterful educators have written stacks of helpful books, articles, and blogs on these teaching structures and we will point you in the direction of many, many resources that you can use to learn more.

Workshop Structure

The first teaching structure to know well and place in your toolbox is a workshop model. A workshop is a longer chunk of time that includes a focus lesson, independent work time, often some collaboration, and a share. The workshop teaching structure was pioneered by Donald Graves, Lucy Calkins, Katie Wood Ray, and many others. This model balances direct instruction with productive practice. In a workshop, students spend the bulk of their time working independently, engaged in authentic reading, writing, science, math, or social studies. Although the students are working on their own, the teacher is in turbo-drive, meeting with small groups built off assessing and observing students, conferring with children one-on-one in responsive emergent ways, and keeping the workshop humming. This instructional model gives students the time and strategies to do the messy work of constructing knowledge and skills and the teacher the time and flexibility to meet the needs of all of his students.

The planning of all these different structures can feel overwhelming. But hang in there, the following planning tool makes the organization of your time much easier. This chart comes courtesy of Jennifer Serravallo's incredibly helpful and handy book *Teaching Reading in Small Groups* (2010) and can easily be adapted to almost any workshop. For more on how the small groups and conferring goals were planned, see "Making and Using a Checklist" on page 114 in the previous section.

SAMPLE TEACHER SCHEDULE DURING A KINDERGARTEN WRITING WORKSHOP

	MONDAY	TUESDAY	WEDNESDAY	THURSDAY	FRIDAY
Focus lesson (planned from resources and looking at student work)	Launch independent writing projects: We get ideas by thinking of books we want in the world.	Build stamina/ add more: Add to your pictures and add to your words.	Build stamina/ add more: Use speech bubbles in your pictures and words.	Build stamina/ add more: Use small actions in your pictures and words.	No lesson

INDEPENDENT WORK TIME

	MONDAY	TUESDAY	WEDNESDAY	THURSDAY	FRIDAY
Small groups (planned off checklist and student work)	None	Stretch words: Micah Jack Lettie Arjun	Add more details to pictures: Princess Lexie Max Jordan	Stretch words: Micah Jack Lettie Arjun	Add more details to pictures: Princess Lexie Max Jordan
One-to-one conferring (responsive to the child's work in the moment)	Harry Anna Ray	Mira Malini Sidney	Ernie Phillippe Jaxson	Micah Benji Jordan	(Student sign-up)
Check-ins (follow up from other conferences or small groups)	Mila Kevin Grace		Micah Lettie Harry	Lexie Ray	Anna Arjun
Share (TBD based on the work children do each day)					

During a workshop, your students may be engaged in a unit of study. A unit of study is a set of lessons that moves a class along a progression for a set of skills. A math unit of study in third grade might focus on division strategies and include many different opportunities for students to experiment with, invent, and share different ways to solve division problems. Within those larger goals, there are a multitude of microprogressions. If you were to step into a workshop, you'd notice that no two children would be working on exactly the same thing. In a first-grade writing workshop, if the class is in the midst of a unit of study of all-about (informational) books, one student might be writing page after page on Mars with diagrams, labels, and a plethora of facts and descriptions, and another is working on a very simple book all about babies. Though these two pieces of writing would look very different (and in fact the teacher's goals for these students would be different, too) each of these students would be taking "just-right" risks and learning and growing—sitting side by side in their writing workshop. And each of these students would be learning to be more independent, highly engaged in their writing, and finding joy in the process of learning.

POSSIBLE UNITS OF STUDY

AREA OF STUDY	POTENTIAL UNITS OF STUDY	PLACES TO FIND MORE
SOCIAL STUDIES	The Neighborhood The American Revolution Community Workers Immigration	*The Curious Classroom: 10 Structures for Teaching with Student-Directed Inquiry* by Harvey Daniels (2017) *From Inquiry to Action: Civic Engagement with Project-Based Learning in All Content Areas* by Steve Zemelman (2016) *Choice Time: How to Deepen Learning Through Inquiry and Play* by Renée Dinnerstein (2016)
MATH	Building Structures/ Geometry Counting and Cardinality Fractions	*Math on the Move: Engaging Students in Whole Body Learning* by Malke Rosenfeld (2016) The Math in Practice series by Sue O'Connell et al. (2016) The Young Mathematicians at Work series by Catherine Twomey Fosnot and Maarten Dolk (2001, 2002)
READING	Reading Information Books Studying Characters Building Reading Habits	*Notice & Note: Strategies for Close Reading* by Kylene Beers and Bob Probst (2012) *Book Love: Developing Depth, Stamina, and Passion in Adolescent Readers* by Penny Kittle (2012) *I Am Reading: Nurturing Young Children's Meaning Making and Joyful Engagement with Any Book* by Kathy Collins and Matt Glover (2015) Units of Study for Teaching Reading, Grade K–5 series by Lucy Calkins and colleagues (2015)
WRITING	Writing Information Books Writing with Elaboration and Craft Independent Writing Projects	*Independent Writing: One Teacher—Thirty-Two Needs, Topics, and Plans* by Colleen Cruz (2004) Units of Study in Opinion, Information, and Narrative Writing, Grades K–5 series by Lucy Calkins and colleagues (2016) *Writing with Mentors: How to Reach Every Writer in the Room Using Current, Engaging Mentor Texts* by Allison Marchetti and Rebecca O'Dell (2015) Anything written by Katie Wood Ray

Here are the basic structures of the workshop model:

STRUCTURE	COMPONENTS
FOCUS LESSON	These lessons gather students together as a class in a meeting area. This can be a time to deliver direct instruction on a strategy, engage in a whole-group inquiry, or use storytelling to teach a lesson. One of your goals for focus lessons should be that they can be useful to *all* of your learners, no matter where they are along a progression of skills. These lessons can highlight the habits and strategies writers, readers, mathematicians, and scientists use. For more on focus lessons, see page 122.
WORK TIME: INDEPENDENT*	During work time, students work independently on the content of the workshop. In a reading workshop, they read or storytell. In a writing workshop, they write, research, rehearse or revise. During a science workshop they experiment, observe, and record. In math, children might be engaged in an investigation, working on a problem set, or playing games. Teachers meet with students in small groups and one-on-one.
WORK TIME: COLLABORATIVE*	Workshops also offer students an opportunity to engage in collaborative, social learning. During this time, the teacher acts as a coach, listening in and meeting with clubs and partnerships, and supports not just the content of what children are learning but the language and social skills as well.
SHARE/ WRAP-UP	At the end of a lesson, the class gathers back at the rug and the workshop concludes.

*Note: These do not have to be distinct times; you just may want to ensure kids work in both ways.

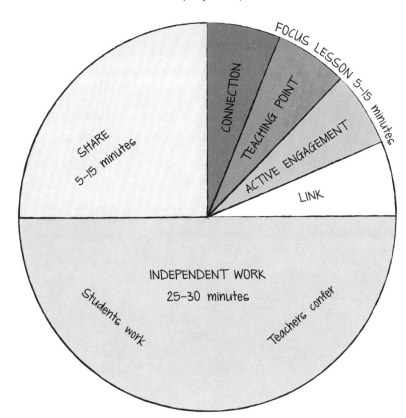

For more see:
- *The Art of Teaching Writing* by Lucy Calkins (1994)
- *The Art of Teaching Reading* by Lucy Calkins (2000)
- *The Reading Workshop: Creating Space for Readers* by Frank Serafini (2001)
- *Growing Readers: Units of Study in the Primary Classroom* by Kathy Collins (2004)
- *About the Authors: Writing Workshop with Our Youngest Writers* by Katie Wood Ray and Lisa Cleaveland (2004)
- *Already Ready: Nurturing Writers in Preschool and Kindergarten* by Katie Wood Ray and Matt Glover (2008)
- *A Place for Wonder: Reading and Writing Nonfiction in the Primary Grades* by Georgia Heard and Jennifer McDonough (2009)
- *Writing Workshop: The Essential Guide* by Ralph Fletcher and JoAnn Portalupi (2001)
- *What Are the Rest of My Kids Doing? Fostering Independence in the K-2 Reading Workshop* by Lindsey Moses and Meridith Ogden (2017)
- *Projecting Possibilities for Writers: The How, What, and Why of Designing Units of Study, K-5* by Matt Glover and Mary Alice Berry (2012).

Focus Lessons

Focus lessons gather the class together at a meeting area to engage in a brief (8–15 minutes!) whole-group experience. These lessons happen at the beginning of each workshop, and we find that our best teaching happens when we find a balance between student-driven inquiry, direct instruction, and storytelling. Teachers select one style that best matches the teaching they wish to do or the support children might need on a given day.

STRUCTURE	FORMAT	SOUNDS LIKE
DIRECT INSTRUCTION	A strategy is modeled by the teacher (with specific steps) and the students practice right there at the lesson. Often children are seated next to partners that they can turn to and talk with and practice the new skill.	**Connection:** Mathematicians, *we've been working on* subtraction strategies. We have a few strategies in our toolkits! **Teaching point:** *Today I want to teach you* that one way mathematicians solve subtraction problems is by subtracting back on an open number line. **Demonstration:** *Watch as I* subtract 32 from 48. *First*, I'll draw a quick number line. *Second*, I'll put 48 on the number line. *Next*, I'll start by subtracting 30 to get to 18. *Finally*, I subtract 2 to get to 16. **Guided practice:** *Let's try it together.* If the problem is 65 - 14, how do I start? *Turn and talk with your partner* and sketch it on your whiteboard. *Next*, we subtract back; what could we subtract first? *Finally*, we subtract the last part of the number. *Turn and talk* to your partner—is this correct? How do you know? **Link:** Mathematicians, when you're solving subtraction problems, you could try this new strategy.
STORYTELLING	The teacher—or a student!—tells a story and the class draws tips, strategies, or inspiration from the story.	One day, Emma was stuck on a math problem. She tried over and over and over again to solve it. Every time she tried to solve it, she got a different answer. It just didn't make sense. Emma was getting more and more frustrated. She took a deep breath and said to herself, "Emma, it's time to be flexible. Is there another way you know to solve this kind of problem?" Emma looked up at the "Subtraction Strategies" chart and—aha!—saw another way. She gave it a try, and sure enough, it worked! When you're feeling stuck, you can use Emma's self-talk. Ask yourself, "Is there another way?" and use the tools around you in the classroom.
INQUIRY	The class comes together to investigate a book, photograph, video, or piece of student work with a guiding question. Partners turn and talk and, ultimately, the class comes to some kind of answer to the question posed.	We've been working on subtracting back on the number line, but Kate did something differently. Does it make sense? Can it work mathematically? *Let's study this and figure out what is going on.*

REASON FOR CHOOSING	FOR MORE INFORMATION	

REASON FOR CHOOSING

To introduce a new strategy that the majority of your students could benefit from.

To showcase the work and thinking of one student and use it as an example for other students.

As one part of a progression of lessons in a unit of study.

FOR MORE INFORMATION

The Art of Teaching Reading (2000) and *The Art of Teaching Writing* (1994) by Lucy Calkins

Units of Study series by Lucy Calkins and colleagues

Whole-Class Teaching: Minilessons and More by Janet Angelillo (2008)

Watch Christine teach a fourth-grade focus lesson on self-talk.

hein.pub/kidsfirst-login

To help build your students' capacity for metacognition (thinking about their thinking). Stories build neural pathways in our brains, and hearing the story of a classmate can give other students suggestions for what to do when they find themselves in similar situations.

A Mindset For Learning: Teaching the Traits of Joyful, Independent Growth by Kristine Mraz and Christine Hertz (2015)

Oral Mentor Texts: A Powerful Tool for Teaching Reading, Writing, Speaking, and Listening by Connie Dierking and Sherra Jones (2014)

To engage children in a constructivist approach to learning where instead of directly teaching the strategy, they are discovering the strategy for themselves.

Inquiry focus lessons can be either teacher driven (highlighting a new idea or strategy you'd like the class to focus on) or student driven (coming together as a class to answer one of their Why? But how? Or I Wonder . . . questions).

A Place for Wonder: Reading and Writing Nonfiction in the Primary Grades by Georgia Heard and Jennifer McDonough (2009)

The Curious Classroom: 10 Structures for Teaching with Student-Directed Inquiry by Harvey "Smokey" Daniels (2017)

Work Time Structures: Small Groups

The small groups you teach in your classroom will be a mix of carefully planned out, ongoing, and highly structured learning opportunities and quick, on-the-fly responses to what you're seeing in the moment in your classroom. *Quick* is an important word here—these lessons should last from ten to fifteen minutes and should have only three to five students in each small group. During the course of a reading workshop, you might be pulling together an impromptu group at the rug to check in about engagement, running two guided reading groups at two different reading levels, and teaching a strategy group on word-solving strategies. To be clear, this juggling act will not come easily or early to your teaching career. We advocate starting with conferring and building up to groups. Then, as your comfort level grows, you will find yourself being more selective in the types of groups you choose for each child. You will also find some children don't fit into any group at certain times; don't force a group! Keep your conferring up and going for those children who have needs that aren't so easily grouped.

Different teachers fit in conferring and small groups in different ways. Kristi starts with her small groups so her children have some time to get into their work before she heads off to confer. Other teachers might confer with one or two children before pulling a group, and then finish with one more conference. Find the rhythm that works for you. Teaching involves trial and error, and error, and error, until you land on something that works for you. The key is to know that one kind of teaching will not be a match for all children. Guided reading is not the right choice for every child, every day. Use the column "Reason for Choosing" to help you think about what structure might support each child in her learning journey.

One way to go about this comes from Jennifer Serravallo's book *Teaching Reading in Small Groups* (2010). Jennifer suggests thinking about the amount of time you have during your workshop work time (anywhere from twenty to forty-five minutes) and then schedule your time. If a small group goes for about ten minutes and conferences for about five, how many of each can you do? The goal is to meet with every child one time a week, not one time a day. And you may meet with some children two or three times a week. We don't advocate trying to meet with any one child every day because kids need some time to work without a teacher breathing actively down their neck. Think about the last really hard exercise class you went to; it was nice when the instructor gave you some breathing room to approximate.

If at this point you are wondering what the other kids are doing as you disco dance your way through small groups and conferences, sit tight, that is coming up.

STRUCTURE	FORMAT	SOUNDS LIKE	REASON FOR CHOOSING	FOR MORE INFORMATION
GUIDED READING	This group starts with a book introduction, then students quickly start reading the same book. While they're reading, the teacher coaches them or takes a running record of their reading. Then, based on what the teacher has observed or on a pre-planned strategy, she teaches a lesson to the group.	Today we are going to read a book called *The Go-Carts* (Randell, Giles, Smith 1996). In this book, the go-carts will have a race, and you will see lots of different-color go-carts. One of them will win! I can't wait to see who! As you read, remember that the picture can help you with the tricky words!	To help move readers between reading levels when they are right on the cusp of transitioning, as evidenced by running records.	*Guided Reading: Responsive Teaching Across the Grades* by Irene Fountas and Gay Su Pinnell (2016) For more on running records: *Literacy Lessons Designed for Individuals* by Marie Clay (2016)
STRATEGY GROUP	These groups bring children together to work on a specific strategy, even if they are reading at different levels or have different goals in writing. Much like a minilesson, a strategy lesson names a specific strategy and gives students the steps that make up that strategy. After the teacher has named the teaching point, he will provide time for demonstration and guided practice, as well.	We've come together because you have all been using the first letter to help you with the words you don't know—what a great strategy! But today I want to teach you that another strategy for solving these words is to think about what word would make sense, or what could fit there. Let's give it a try.	To support students with a specific strategy, no matter their level (e.g., retelling or reading fluently).	*Teaching Reading in Small Groups: Differentiated Instruction for Building Strategic, Independent Readers* by Jennifer Serravallo (2010)
SHARED EXPERIENCE	Gather a group of students together to work collaboratively. They take turns working toward a single goal such as writing a shared story, reading a song, solving a math problem, or analyzing a poem.	Today we're going to read this wonderful book together, *Worm Is Stuck* (Caple 2000). Poor worm! Just look at him. I'll read it first, and then we'll read it together, just like we do as a class during shared reading, and really work on making our voices match the story. Let's get started . . .	Shared experiences are more open-ended small groups. They include interactive writing and small-group inquiries. They can even support students to problem solve during a choice time. These small groups offer a low-stakes way to practice, with plenty of guidance from the teacher.	*Comprehension and Collaboration: Inquiry Circles for Curiosity, Engagement, and Understanding* by Stephanie Harvey and Harvey "Smokey" Daniels (2015)
INDEPENDENT COACHING	A less formal small group, independent coaching allows the teacher to coach into a small group of students as they work independently.	Readers, you've been practicing all of your strategies for solving puzzling words. Keep on reading on your own and when I pop around to you, let me listen in a bit. Let's get to reading!	This small group scaffolds students' independent use of the strategies they've learned. The teacher can work with a group of students and offer quick tips or reminders.	*Prompting Guide* by Irene C. Fountas and Gay Su Pinnell (2017)

Work Time: Conferences

Conferences offer teachers that hard-to-carve-out, oh-so-sweet, one-on-one time with students. All great teaching starts with connection. Sitting down to confer with a child offers an opportunity for relationship building and a chance for the child to feel heard. Conferences

STRUCTURE	FORMAT	SOUNDS LIKE
TEACHING CONFERENCE	The teacher and student sit side by side. The teacher researches the student's work (asks questions, looks closely at writing/reading/math, etc.). Then, the teacher compliments something the student is doing well and provides one little teaching tip. The teacher models the tip and then the student practices while the teacher coaches.	**Research:** How's it going? What are you working on today? Can I take a look at your writing? **Compliment:** I'm noticing that you're adding in lots of dialogue. The dialogue really brings your story to life. I can hear the emotion in your voice, the sadness. Wow! It's powerful. **Teach:** One other tip I have for you as a writer is that in addition to using dialogue to really bring your story to life, you can also use specific language to describe what your body was doing in that moment. **Model:** Let's give it a try. Take a look at this part right here. Show me what your body looked like when you said this. Great! Let's write that in. **Practice:** OK, now you can give it a try. Find another place in your writing where we could put in a little body language clue. **Link:** By adding in a little hint about your body language now and then, you give your reader an even stronger image of the story.
GOAL-SETTING CONFERENCE	This conference is very similar to the teaching conference, but here the teacher and student work collaboratively to set a goal for the student's next steps. Although the teacher may guide the student toward a goal, the student still has agency and choice over the ultimate decision.	Your story is really coming along! How do you think it's going? It seems like you have a really solid first draft and that now might be a good time to set a goal for what you'll work on. Let's talk about what's going really well for you as a writer. What's tricky for you as a writer? Let's pick just one of those tricky things—adding different kinds of details, writing a lot in one workshop, or adding in punctuation. Which would you like to work on?
COACHING CONFERENCE	In a coaching conference, the teacher will sit next to the student and offer tips and reminders as they work. Instead of teaching something new, the teacher uses this time as a chance to nudge the student toward the tools and strategies they have already been introduced to.	Today as you write, I'm just going to check in every now and again with some quick reminders and tips. I can't wait to see what you write! Let's get started. Hmm. Are you trying to spell a word you don't know? What could you do? Don't forget: all of those great drawings from your picture can be in your words, too! Wow! Nice dialogue. Who said that? Was it you or your sister?

also offer an opportunity to custom fit your teaching to offer the precise little nudge that each student needs next. In one conference you might offer a specific teaching point, and in another you might help a child set a meaningful goal, and in another still you might just coach the child along as they work.

REASON FOR CHOOSING	FOR MORE INFORMATION
Teaching conferences offer highly responsive, direct instruction for students. They allow the teacher to build on something the student is doing already, or something the student is "using and confusing." Teaching conferences also offer opportunities to reinforce strategies that have been introduced in a minilesson in a one-on-one setting.	*Conferring with Readers: Supporting Each Student's Growth and Independence* by Jennifer Serravallo and Gravity Goldberg (2007) *One to One: The Art of Conferring with Young Writers* by Lucy Calkins, Amanda Hartman, and Zoë Ryder White (2005) *How's It Going? A Practical Guide to Conferring with Student Writers* by Carl Anderson (2000)
Goal-setting conferences help build students' agency and autonomy in their learning. After the goal has been picked, you can check in regularly with the student and provide just a bit of support, as needed. Goal-setting conferences can be a means to build learning habits or to set content-specific goals.	*The Reading Strategies Book: Your Everything Guide to Developing Skilled Readers* (2015) and *The Writing Strategies Book: Your Everything Guide to Developing Skilled Writers* (2017) by Jennifer Serravallo
A coaching conference is similar to an independent coaching small group, but can be especially useful one-on-one as a way to differentiate and support students at all levels.	*DIY Literacy: Teaching Tools for Differentiation, Rigor, and Independence* by Kate Roberts and Maggie Beattie Roberts (2016)

Watch Christine coach a first grader in a reading goal-setting conference.

hein.pub/kidsfirst-login

Reflective Conversations

Reflection drives growth. When you've finished cooking a new recipe for the first time, you pause to think, *How did that go?* and *What worked? What didn't? What would I do differently?* When something goes beautifully, you want to celebrate it with everyone at your table (and maybe the world, thanks, Instagram!) and when something flops, you want to get to the bottom of why it didn't work out. The same is true for our students: the moments when we gather as a class for reflection and conversation celebrate, solidify, and propel their learning.

STRUCTURE	FORMAT	SOUNDS LIKE	REASON FOR CHOOSING	FOR MORE INFORMATION
SHARES Watch Christine coach a fourth grader through a student-led share. hein.pub/kidsfirst-login 	At the end of a workshop period, the class gathers back together to reflect on the work students have just done. Shares can be teacher led, student led, or led by a partnership or small group. These gatherings are brief—usually only five to seven minutes, but are very valuable.	• (The skill or strategy addressed in the focus lesson is reinforced.) Jenna used the pictures to figure out the word *snow*, just like we practiced at our minilesson. Let's all watch what Jenna did. • (A student or a group of students shares something from their independent or collaborative time.) Matt wrote and rewrote this section of his narrative using several different writing moves. Let's study his work. • (A habit or skill is reinforced with a story or example.) Malcolm used flexibility to solve that long division problem. One way didn't work, so he tried another way. Let's study how Malcolm was flexible.	The type of share a teacher chooses can be based on carefully laid-out plans, or can be a very responsive, spur-of-the-moment decision based on what she is seeing in a workshop.	*Don't Forget to Share: The Crucial Last Step in the Writing Workshop* by Leah Mermelstein (2007)
GRAND CONVERSATIONS Watch Kristi introduce grand conversations to a first-grade class. hein.pub/kidsfirst-login	The whole class sits together—often in a circle—and has a conversation. The teacher aims to be as removed as possible and often is physically outside the circle. The class discusses a situation, a question, a provocation, etc., and tries to draw some kind of conclusion or reveal an idea.	We're going to pause our math workshop right here and have a grand conversation. So many of you found this problem tricky today, and that's OK! Let's try to learn from this situation. What can we do when things get really, really tricky? Who would like to start?	These whole-class conversations are excellent opportunities to develop students' speaking and listening skills. They also build the class community and collaborative culture.	*Talking Their Way into Science: Hearing Children's Questions and Theories, Responding with Curricula* by Karen Gallas (1995) *A Mindset for Learning: Teaching the Traits of Joyful, Independent Growth* by Kristine Mraz and Christine Hertz (2015)

Burning Question Answered: But What Are Kids Doing When I Am Running This Whole Thing?

Short unsatisfying answer: their own work.

Longer, possibly more satisfying answer: The key to workshop is the word *work*. Not busywork or centers, but authentic, meaningful work. So when you are working with kids in groups and one-on-one in reading, the rest of the kids are reading books that are just right for them. In writing, kids are writing books based on their interests and topics they care about. In math, children are playing math games or completing investigations or tackling questions. All of this happens *independently*, meaning without you, but with the support of peers and partners.

Most often we hear that when teachers aren't "supervising," kids aren't working. We think this comes down to a few factors.

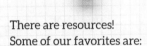

There are resources! Some of our favorites are:

- *Growing Readers: Units of Study in the Primary Classroom* by Kathy Collins (2004)

- Units of Study for Teaching Reading, Grades K–5 series by Lucy Calkins and colleagues (2015)

- Units of Study in Opinion, Information, and Narrative Writing, Grades K–5 series by Lucy Calkins and colleagues (2016)

- *What Are the Rest of My Kids Doing? Fostering Independence in the K–2 Reading Workshop* by Lindsey Moses and Meridith Ogden (2017)

- ★ Start slow and build up. The first workshop should only be as long as it's productive, then add minute by minute.

- ★ Teach how to resolve issues independently. What do I do when I'm stuck? What if my pen breaks? What if I need something? Your environment will help support this independence, which is why materials need to be easily accessible for your children.

- ★ Keep conferences and small groups short at the start. Very short.

- ★ Trust that noise is productive. Silent work is not necessarily good; kids might need to talk to make sense of what they are doing. Set protocols and limits on how that might sound.

- ★ Make sure kids are engaged in meaningful work. Kids can smell busywork a mile off; don't try to keep them busy, keep them engaged by asking them to take on big projects, like writing their own books, or reading things they care about.

Incorporate Reflection into Your Practice

Teachers spend years practicing, studying, flailing through these teaching structures. There's a lot of truth to the cliché that teachers are lifelong learners. Even after years of teaching and coaching, both Kristi and Christine find themselves wrapping up a small group or a conference thinking, "Well, that was a flop" or "Well, that was surprisingly effective!" Take time to try to figure out exactly why something fell flat or went well. We can learn from what we feel are our failures and what we see as our teaching glory moments. The beauty of working with a group of children for a year is that we don't have to aim for perfection, just progress. And when you still can't put your finger on why your students—or one particular student—isn't meeting a goal, it may be time to take a look at some other factors. In the next section, we'll tackle how time, level of preference, group size, and degree of familiarity can all have a powerful effect on your students' engagement and growth.

Big Idea: Responsive Teachers Draw from All They Know

Chefs Know Ingredients, Not Just Recipes

Do you ever watch competitive cooking shows like *Chopped* or *Top Chef*? These shows often spring a surprise ingredient or set of ingredients on experienced chefs, and ask them to create a meal. The secret to performing well, it seems to us, is to know ingredients well. What pairs together? How do you cook asparagus? What flavors are brought out when fennel is fried? If you only ever know recipes, it becomes difficult to innovate when a problem pops up. Knowing your ingredients, and how to manipulate them, allows a chef to think on her feet, invent and experiment, and make a feast out of any basket of random ingredients.

This seems to us cooking show addicts to be a pretty apt metaphor for teaching. The better you know your stuff (as we pros call it), the better you can create learning experiences for your children. So what comprises "stuff"? What are the variables that fall under our control? How do we build and remove scaffolds to learning for our kiddos? Well, tie that apron on tight, because that's what we intend to figure out here.

Differentiation Is Your Friend

One buzzword that teachers hear a lot is *differentiation*. As in "How will you differentiate for your students?" or "What is your plan for differentiation in this lesson?" Before we actually knew what that word meant, we went for the easy play of, "Uh, I will differentiate by making it different." Lots of curricula offer differentiation options in the form of "bonus problems" or suggestions like, "If the child has difficulty, offer manipulatives." This is certainly a kind of differentiation, mainly around content. I can give children different numbers in math to scale the problem harder or easier. I can give children different levels of books to ensure they are doing powerful reading and thinking work. But, too often differentiation stops at the content level, and yet children still need something different to be successful.

Beyond Changing Content

Kristen GoldMansour is an inclusion consultant extraordinaire who works with teachers in their classrooms and with their teaching practice. Kristi had the pleasure of working with Kristen when she was the special educator in a kindergarten inclusion classroom. Kristen was helping Kristi puzzle out some supports for a child who was experiencing challenges when she drew a quick visual kind of like this:

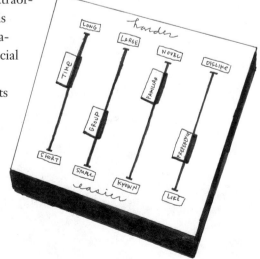

The very wise Kristen helped Kristi understand that teachers often don't realize all the factors that are in play for students at any given time. From who the child is sitting with to what the child is sitting on can be elements that contribute to a child's success, or lack thereof. A teacher who is truly matching instruction to children looks at the factors that affect a whole child, not just the content. Too often many of these factors are permanently set on high. Kristen's explanation of the factors and how they could be manipulated was fairly earth shattering. After Kristi recovered from the small earthquake that visual provoked on a neurological level, she set to thinking about differentiation in a much bigger way. What follows is our interpretation of this huge idea that Kristen shared.

Looking Closer at Classroom Factors

Early in this book, we talked about how seating could be differentiated, and in the same way a just-right seat can enable a child to work and play at higher levels, these same variables can help a child become successful without ever changing the content of the work the child is asked to do. All of these factors can be looked at as ways to differentiate for individual children, groups of children, or as temporary adjustments for a whole class. The goal in all of this is to adjust each factor until a child is successful, and then slowly increase the difficulty levels a bit at a time, maintaining success along the way. You will be asked to do a bit of determining importance here, and we'll think through that after going through each factor.

Time Frame: Doing something for a shorter amount of time is often easier than doing something for a longer amount of time. We don't mean in a testing, timed situation where you are asked to complete a set in a short time. It is definitely not any easier to run a mile in six minutes than it is in fifteen. Instead, think about going to the gym. It's much easier to work out for fifteen minutes than an hour when you are trying to get back in shape. And sometimes working out for fifteen minutes gives you the confidence to go at it for a little longer next time. Likewise, in the classroom, a forty-five-minute writing time may, for some children, result in writing that seems disorganized or sparse, but when the time is reduced to twenty minutes, the child's writing is much more successful. The issue for this child is not the content, but rather the duration of the task. Rather than teaching and reteaching how to organize, we can play with the factor of time. Building in breaks and slowly increasing stamina will help this child build the skill he needs: endurance in writing. The issue for this child was never the act of writing.

Group Size: Working and learning in smaller groups will tend to be easier than acquiring the same information or completing the same task in a large group. Think about the college courses you had in a lecture hall versus the more intimate, desks-in-a-circle kind of class you may have had. What can happen in larger groups? Your attention fades; you lose the thread of the lesson; you are distracted by the doodles in the notebook of the person in front of you or the constant nose sniffling of the undergrad next to you. Sometimes the challenge for a student is not that she could not understand your teaching, but she could not assimilate the information while seated behind a child with a hair bow she was dying to touch. Teaching the same content in a smaller group might be all that child needs to be successful. Distractions will be fewer, engagement with the material and the teacher will be higher, and the child can work on focus and self-regulation in large groups over time.

Degree of Familiarity: You know how it's always easier to drive to a place you have been before than a place that is brand-new? Well, the same is true for learning. Familiarity can be about content ("Ahh, I've seen something like this before"), which is why we activate prior knowledge, but it can also be about people and locations. For some children, working with unfamiliar peers could be the cause of their struggle. Their social anxiety might be such that even sitting by children they don't know well may impact the work they do. Likewise, novel adults, new seats, unknown topics, a change in schedule, anything new can sap at the ability to be successful. Some children need familiarity to feel safe enough to work, and so ensuring that those children take on new learning in a familiar way with familiar people and a familiar topic may be the best path to success. Having said that, for some children (those explorer play personalities we talked about in Section 1), the novelty is the source of engagement. Knowing your children in multiple ways can help you decide which way to go.

Level of Preference: Not surprisingly, how much you like something can determine how successful you are at it. When we find things pleasurable, we are more likely to improvise, bounce back from setbacks, and perceive it as play rather than work. If I have assigned my writers a topic like "polar bears" and asked them write an all-about book to show what they know, and they are having trouble being successful, the issue could be that the topic or nonfiction genre is nonpreferred. Giving the child free range of topic or genre makes the task easier. The question we have to ask ourselves is, could a child show their learning more effectively given a choice here? If my teaching goal is to see what the child learned about polar bears, where are the choices for the child to demonstrate preference? Maybe in genre—there are poems and stories that teach. Maybe in the choice of sign system. Writing is one way to communicate information, but so is building a polar bear habitat in blocks or creating a dramatic scene about bears. If my goal is to see if the child can write an informational book, why does it have to be about polar bears? It could be written about fairies, Pokémon, the laundromat or whatever else the child has a passion for.

Children can have preferences physically (where they sit, the tools they use) and temperamentally (the people they are with, the time of day they do work, the topics they learn about). Allowing children to work in preferred ways is a form of differentiation. We are not suggesting teachers never set parameters, but when setting limits on what children can do, critically consider why, then activate your flexible teacher stance and play with the variables children can have ownership over.

Determining Importance: What Is the Most Meaningful Challenge for Each Child?

In a classroom where teachers are not aware of all the subtle ways to create different learning paths for children, all of these factors might be set on the hardest level. Children might be asked to work for a long time, in a large group, on new and nonpreferred content. Even in this "all dials on high" setting some children will be successful. However, it is the children who encounter difficulty that intrigue us at this moment. Is the issue the content—for example, the math strategy or the reading skill or the writing technique—or is it one of those other factors? And what is the *most important* work for the child to be doing at this moment? Ryan Dunn, math coach extraordinaire, taught us that everything we teach has a social goal, language goal, and content goal, and we cannot just plan for one. For some children, the most important work might be building their language; others might have social goals, like turn taking, that supersede learning the content at that moment; and others might need to focus on learning the content of the lesson. For more specific suggestions on meeting the needs of English language learners, check out our interview with Yvonne Yiu on page 141.

Likewise, if we determine that a child's most important work in reading is stamina, or the length of time he can read, and not the actual act of reading, we may for a brief time give the child a mix of easier or shorter books and frequent breaks as we work with the him to read for longer and longer periods of time. At this moment, the teacher is less concerned with the push toward harder books and skills and more concerned with the ability to sustain reading for long periods. As the child's stamina grows, we then may shift the child back into harder and longer books.

Sometimes the most important thing is learning the content of the lessons, but sometimes it is building skills in one of the other factors: handling novel tasks, working in nonpreferred ways, learning and working in large groups. Our task as teachers is to figure out which areas we are working on building with the child and manipulate the amount of challenge in the other factors so he can be successful. Then, as one area grows, we lift the level of challenge in another. Slowly and methodically we adjust what we can to ensure children face just-right classroom challenges.

Snapshots of Differentiation in a Third-Grade Writing Workshop

How does this play out in a classroom? Let's visit the room of Kathryn Cazes and Molly Murray, two third-grade teachers who teach in an ICT (coteaching classroom). Forty percent of their students have special needs, and the other 60 percent do not. Differentiation is not for those with special needs alone; within this classroom a multitude of small shifts are made to ensure all students are successful. Let's take a quick look at how the writing workshop is different for a few children, depending on the area of growth identified.

Bulk of Students
Unit: Personal Essay

At this time of year, students are working in writers' notebooks to plan and draft personal essays on topics of their choosing. Their focused lesson is done on a rug for about fifteen minutes, and then the children have about forty-five minutes of uninterrupted writing time. Writing is done in pen, in a composition notebook, at seats of the student's choosing.

Alena
Goal: Write a Personal Essay with Detail (Content)

Alena's goal is to write a personal essay, similar in content to that of her peers, but visually different, meaning it will be of shorter length and with pictures to carry some of her meaning. Alena has difficulty in expressive and receptive language, so the teachers have ensured an access point through the use of illustrations in her writing, almost like a graphic novel. To make this work more successful for her, Molly and Kathryn have made several accommodations to support her during writing time. First, Alena receives a quick recap in a small group at the end of the focus lesson when others go off to work. She has a list of pregenerated, familiar essay topics that she made with a teacher. Alena is not writing in a composition notebook, but instead has paper with boxes at the top for illustrating her ideas before she writes. Finally, Alena sits with a preferred partner who can serve as a go-to when she encounters questions or issues. Though Alena's work will not look exactly like that of her classmates, she is still achieving the goal of writing a personal essay.

Miles

Goal: Build Stamina to Write for Forty-Five Minutes (Time Frame)

Miles can write with high levels of competency, but he tires quickly both physically and mentally. Before structures were put in place to support Miles, his work would often look messy, disorganized, and confusing. To support Miles in building his stamina, Kathryn and Molly developed a plan for him. Miles sits in a chair using a slant board at the table in front of him and has a specialized writing utensil to support his fine motor work. He also has access to work on a computer. Next to him, Miles has a schedule and a timer that help him manage his time. Miles' expected work time is seven minutes, followed by a three-minute break, repeatedly, until the end of the period. Because the content of the learning is not the issue, no changes have been made to his topics, group size, or the form his writing will take.

Oskar

Goal: Attend and Work in Larger Groups (Group Size)

Oskar has demonstrated a great deal of proficiency when instruction occurs in small groups; his teachers are currently trying to build his capacity for self-regulation and attention in the larger-group focus lesson. Oskar sits by a preferred and familiar friend on the rug and holds a fidget to help him stay focused. His teachers have placed him near the front of the rug and use visuals and model topics of high engagement with Oskar to help him maintain focus during the fifteen-minute lessons. Because this attention can exhaust Oskar, he takes a quick body break after the lesson and then checks in with his familiar and preferred friend when he comes back in to make sure he did not miss any additional directions. Because Oskar can lose focus when working at a table with a large group of children, he has a writing area that he has individualized and that is more private.

Among the others in the classroom, one can see children sitting on flexible seating, working on clipboards, taking breaks, and generally following an individualized path to success. This is differentiation at its core.

Building (and Removing) Scaffolds

A word that is often paired with differentiation is *scaffold*. Sometimes it's a verb, as in, "How will you scaffold that learning?" and sometimes as a noun, as in, "What scaffolds do you have in place to support the learner?" But what is it? A scaffold is a temporary (say that nine times in a row), *temporary* support to help a child access a specific skill or aspect of the curriculum. For example, for a child who is disorganized in the morning, a scaffold could be an individualized unpacking checklist, or a buddy to help her put everything away, or even a few spaced verbal prompts from an adult when the child completes each step of the morning routine. These supports allow the child to get organized and ready to work in the morning in the same way her peers do. The number one pitfall of scaffolds is when they cease to be temporary and become permanent fixtures in a child's life.

Watch Kristi teach a fourth-grade class about creating a personalized writing schedule.

hein.pub/kidsfirst-login

How to Build a Scaffold

When building a scaffold, the questions we ask can help us determine what it could look like and how the child will use it. Scaffolds should use children's strengths, so a child who has a strong visual sense might benefit from a small chart. Likewise, a child who has a strong social sense might benefit from a buddy to check in with. The idea is that a scaffold uses children's strengths to help them through struggles, and closes the space between what they can do and what they are being asked to do.

Some questions to consider are:

★ What can the child do independently?

★ What is the child being asked to do?

★ What strengths does the child have that can help us build the scaffold?

★ How, when, and why will the scaffold be used?

★ How will I know if the scaffold is working?

★ How will the child know if the scaffold is working?

Examples of Scaffolds

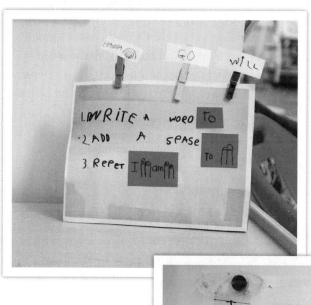

How to Remove a Scaffold

Building a scaffold requires a thoughtful process, and so does removing a scaffold. Just as crutches can help you through a broken leg, a scaffold can help you through a tricky part of learning, but you don't keep crutches forever. Removing scaffolds should be considered as much a process as building them in the first place. Some guiding questions to help you through this part may be:

★ How do I reduce the use or supportiveness of the scaffold over time?

★ How will the child help plan next steps?

★ What is the time frame the child and I expect for the scaffold to be in use? How long will it take to phase the scaffold out?

★ What will the child need to do without the scaffold in place?

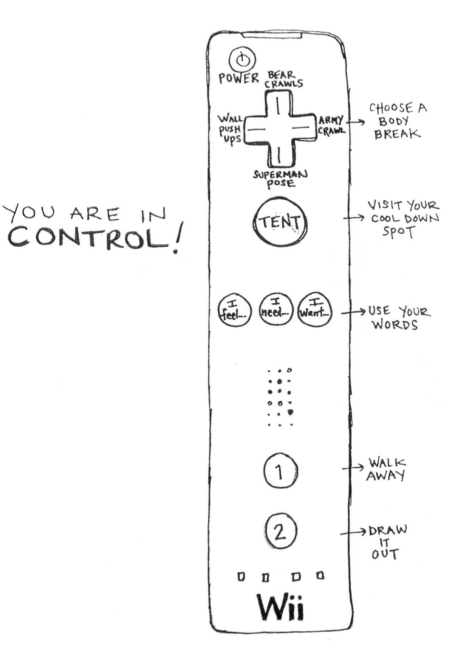

Conclusion: Assume Success Is Possible When the Factors Are Right

According to Harvard researcher Robert Rosenthal, there is a relationship between the expectation a teacher has about a student and what that student will be able to achieve (Spiegel 2012). Let that sink in for a moment.

In even the most trying of circumstances, with even the most trying of students, it's important that we assume that if we keep at it, if we keep observing and modifying and experimenting, then when we get the factors right our students will be successful. We must believe that there is, in fact, always a way. If we hold firm to that assumption, then we must commit to putting in the effort. Though it would be much easier to shrug something off and say, "They'll never get that," that is a false statement. Working through each moment of confusion is the great challenge and, when we finally solve the puzzle, the great reward of teaching.

Annie Dunn is a special educator in Shelburne, Vermont. We asked Annie about what classroom teachers need to know about special education and how they can collaborate with providers.

Q What is an IEP? How do I use it?

A *IEP* stands for an individualized education plan. An IEP is a fluid document created by a team that includes the classroom teacher, special educator, parents/guardians, and other service providers such as an occupational therapist, physical therapist, school psychologist, or behavioral interventionist. When it's appropriate, some students should be a part of their IEP development. An IEP is in effect for an entire calendar year. The team meets yearly to review the IEP and make changes. However, because it is a fluid document, a team can call a meeting at any point and make adjustments as needed.

An IEP is broken up into several different sections. It begins with the student's *present level of performance*. In that section, the student's disability is described, as well as areas of physical, academic, social/emotional strengths and needs. The second section addresses the *student's goals*. In this section, the team creates a list of goals that the student is working towards.

The third section of the IEP outlines what *services* a student needs to make progress. These services can include small-group instruction, one-on-one instruction, speech and language services, observations and consultation, and more. This section identifies the service, the service provider, the location, how often they will meet with the student, and how frequently they will meet with the student.

The final section of an IEP is the *accommodations*. All children learn differently and accommodations are the key to success for many students and adjust how a child learns the content, not the content itself. Accommodations can include:

★ Environment: the setting in which children are learning

★ Time: how long a child has to accomplish a given task

★ Preteaching: introducing a concept or vocabulary, for example, before it's introduced in the whole class

★ Materials and tools: any supports (from something simple such as a visual, to something more complex such as a speech generative device) that allow a child to work with increasing independence. (For more on scaffolds and differentiating, see page 135.)

The goal of accommodations is that we remove the challenge or obstacles so the child can show what they know. This allows students with disabilities to access the regular education and be successful.

"These students are smart and capable. Treat them like that. Have realistic and high expectations; push them."

Q What is the biggest misconception about children with IEPs?

A By definition, individuals with a learning disability do not struggle because of low intelligence, poor teaching, lack of motivation, or other such factors. Most children with specific learning disabilities such as a reading disability or a math calculation disability have average to above average cognitive abilities. Their underachievement is unexpected and unexplained, which is why the term is often misunderstood.

Q What do you wish all teachers knew about children with IEPs?

A These students are smart and capable. Treat them like that. Have realistic and high expectations; push them. They are not lazy; they are actually working really hard, harder than others. Keep in mind that, if they could do it, they would do it. Kids want to do well. It's also important to remember that IEPS are a legal document, not a suggestion. They were created for a reason. If you have suggestions and or questions about an IEP or a goal, reach out to your special educator.

Q What are some tips for teachers on collaborating and communicating with special educators?

A Set up a regular time to meet that you both hold sacred to discuss your student or students. Attend each meeting with some form of data (e.g., a running record) so you have something concrete to focus on—what are we focusing on this week for this child? It's important to create a system for communicating goals, instruction, and progress. Jennifer Serravallo recommends having a folder—similar to a patient's chart at the hospital—where the classroom teacher and the special educator can write notes and keep track of information. Avoid talking about students in front of the children. It can be tempting, because we're all so busy, but children pick up on way more than we think they do. Above all else, see the children on IEPs in your class as *your students*, not just the special educator's students. You're an incredibly vital member of the child's team.

Yvonne Yiu is an ELL teacher in New York City. We took some time to ask her about what classroom teachers need to know about English language learners (ELLs) and how they can collaborate with providers.

Q Who gets ELL services?

A There are two types of students who receive ELL services. The first type of ELL is a student who moved from another country whose first language is a language other than English. The second type of ELL is a student who is born in the United States, but speaks another language at home. Typically, potential ELLs are identified during the school registration process and are given subsequent assessment to determine whether the child needs English support.

Q What are the most common misconceptions about children who are ELLs?

A **"ELL students can't participate."** ELLs can indeed participate with the proper support and opportunity to show their learning and understanding in different ways, not just verbally. Even the youngest and newest ELL students can use gestures, pointing, and drawings to participate and express themselves.

"All ELLs are the same." Although it is true that all ELLs are learning English, what teachers don't always realize is that there are many factors that impact the speed and manner in which their ELLs will learn English, including the level of literacy in the native language, the sounds and grammar of their native language, their prior school environment, cultural communication norms, and individual student personality. Sometimes ELLs do not want to be in the United States at all, and may be resistant to learning English.

"He/(or she) speaks English, and no longer needs support." Sometimes students will surprise their teachers as being classified as ELLs, as they can have conversations in English and interact with their peers in the classroom and on the playground in English. It is important to remember that social language is acquired more quickly than academic language. Advanced-level ELLs need support with academic reading and writing in order to succeed at their grade level.

Q What are some simple things I can do to support ELLs in my classroom?

A **Visuals, visuals, visuals!** Add pictures or photos to charts, schedules, checklists, and word walls. This doesn't just pertain to the lower grades—visuals support all learners and enable access.

Use gestures to communicate meaning. Gestures are especially helpful when giving directions and asking and answering questions. Linking gestures with common phrases or vocabulary can help students learn.

Assign a buddy. It is more important that the buddy be a friendly and patient student than speak the same language.

"Students know whether they are valued and welcomed and can sense if others want them to join in or not. By helping students find similarities with each other and build relationships, ELLs can be happier and more comfortable at school."

Assign turn-and-talk "triads." Putting ELLs in a group of three with two strong students provides them with supportive language models to listen to and the opportunity to join in the conversation without the pressure of needing to "perform."

Activate prior knowledge by showing pictures or videos and having discussions about what your students know about a topic. ELLs all come with prior knowledge and different life experiences. Don't assume your ELLs will know everything your students know, but at the same time, don't assume that your ELLs will know nothing about a topic.

Front-load important vocabulary. When starting a unit, introduce some important vocabulary words that are key to understanding. Before daily lessons, students can also preview words that they'll need for that day.

Use sentence starters. From the simplest "I am . . ." and "I need . . ." for the newest ELL students to those for advanced ELL students that support their use of academic language, sentence starters are a great way to support all students and can be easily differentiated.

Scaffold and differentiate using questioning. ELLs can participate in read-aloud and discussions if they are asked questions that are differentiated for their level. At the newcomer stage, ELLs will be successful with lower-level questioning that enables them to answer with yes or no, choose from two options, or point to something in a picture.

Q What do you wish every teacher knew about ELLs?

A ELLs need to be integrated into the classroom community. Students know whether they are valued and welcomed and can sense if others want them to join in or not. By helping students find similarities with each other and build relationships, ELLs can be happier and more comfortable at school. It's important for ELLs to be physically with the class and engage in class activities with support rather than being isolated on their own doing separate work the entire school day.

ELLs (and all language learners) go through a "silent period" when they are first learning a new language. They may be resistant to repeating phrases or responding verbally to questions. It's a normal stage of language acquisition, and sometimes ELLs who do know some English also go through this phase when they transition to an all-English school environment. The more students feel happy and comfortable at school, the sooner they will be willing to take risks, try out their new English skills, and make progress.

ELLs need emotional support and encouragement. The transition to a new country, school environment, and language is a lot for students to handle. Oftentimes this is even more difficult for students who are used to being at the top of their class in their prior school. Having parents of ELLs talk to their children about how this transition process is temporary and the need to be patient and encouraging them try and show what they know as much as possible is often very helpful.

Kate and Maggie Beattie Roberts are ex middle school teachers, consultants, and authors of the book *DIY Literacy: Teaching Tools for Differentiation, Rigor, and Independence* (2016). You can find more of their work on kateandmaggie.com and follow them on Twitter at @teachkate and @maggiebroberts. We asked them about what classroom teachers need to know about using tools as scaffolds in their classrooms.

Q So, you guys have an amazing book out for teachers called DIY Literacy. Can you tell us what it is about?

A *DIY Literacy* aims to help teachers create responsive, helpful tools for students to use when they are trying to become more independent. It takes on four different types of teaching tools that we can develop that might help get at some of the root issues we see with learning— trouble remembering past teaching, a misunderstanding of what it means to be "rigorous," and not being able to find your footing in the curriculum, ultimately an issue with differentiation.

Q You guys are masters at breaking teaching down into really concrete steps for kids. Can you talk us through that process a little?

A The first thing we suggest to all educators is to put yourself in your students' shoes as much as possible. Whatever you are teaching them to do, do it yourself. Read the books they are reading and try the work you are asking them to try. Write. Do math. Then, begin to do it like them—get to know how they think, read, process, and practice doing the work in ways you see your students doing the work. Often this highlights in neon what it is that kids need next to help them in their learning journey.

We also believe that as teachers we need to develop a hunger for strategies that will help our kids reach the next level of their work. We all know the feeling of sitting with a student and being able to identify what the "problem" is but not being sure of what the solution is. We argue that this is a powerful moment for us—when we don't know what to teach, do we go and find out? Do I hunt for the strategy, or the trick, or the tip, or the metaphor, or the pop culture reference that will unlock the next step for students to try more independently the work we are setting out for them?

Empathizing with our kids and searching for strategies develop our abilities to see the small, concrete steps a kids might take.

Q What kinds of tools do you see a lot in classrooms? What kinds of tools do you wish you saw more of?

A The instructional chart is the most widely known teaching tool, and when used well (or at least used), it is an incredibly useful one.

Generally, it is not the *kind* of tool we would like to see more of, it's the *way* that tools are used in classrooms. In the best classrooms the tools center around, develop from, and are used in concert with the students. They are created because of a need seen in our classes. They are created with our kids in mind and then are taught into over time so that what is on them can become internalized. Tools used in these ways can be truly transformational. In that, we would rather see one chart used over and over again because it serves such a central need for kids rather than a class chockfull of tools no one is using.

Q Can you give us any tips for how to make our classrooms work for all kids?

A Lately, the word that has been surfacing for us is *focus*. Make sure our units focus on a small enough set of skills that we can truly get our arms wrapped around them (and the kids as they practice them). Develop a few tools that feel responsive and that we feel like we can teach into. Assess with this focus in mind. This way, our classrooms might feel a little less like a circus act of spinning a million plates in the air and more like a place where kids come to get better at independently doing important and meaningful work.

— ♡ —

"Whatever you are teaching them to do, do it yourself. Read the books they are reading and try the work you are asking them to try. Write. Do math."

Conclusion

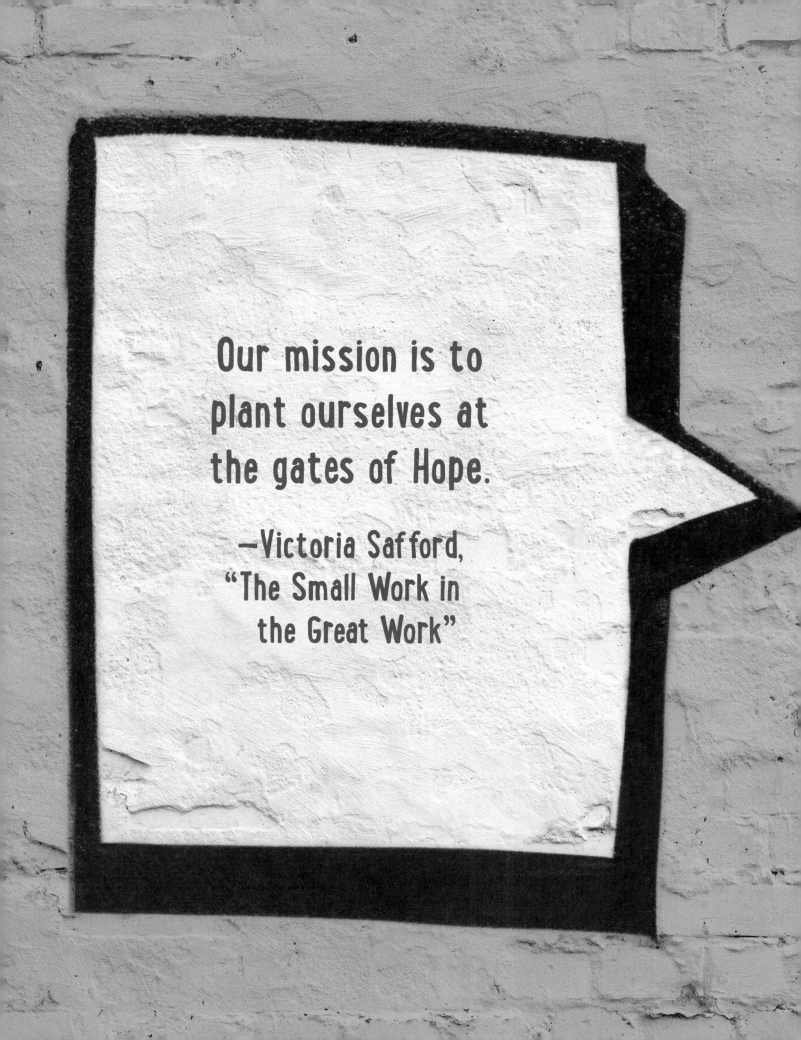

Let's Get to Work

As we conclude this book, we want to make clear that our work together is just beginning. Our hope is that this book serves as a launchpad for work in classrooms around the country and around the world. Our community is a large one—teachers, school leaders, parents, and children with a different vision for what schools and our world could be. Together we say: we believe the change we want to see in the world tomorrow starts in our classrooms today. It could be a reenvisioning of ourselves, our classroom spaces, our ways of interacting with children, or our tools for teaching. We hope as you read, you tugged on a thread that caught your heart and mind and followed it to the other authors, the other resources, and the other teachers growing and working in similar ways. At the core of this heartbreaking, mind-bending work is this community. We are not bound by the four walls of our classrooms anymore, but instead by our vision of what is possible. The "piece of ground from which you see the world both as it is and as it could be, as it will be." You will never be alone in that place.

We believe in agency, empathy, independence, and joy. Joy in the successes, and joy in the struggle. We know that the job is messy, the days are long, but our undertaking couldn't be any more timely or important. So reach out, stay in touch, and come along with us. We've got work to do.

Tips for Family Interaction

1. **Start from the basic assumption that all caregivers are trying to do their best for their child.** For some, this might mean they work multiple jobs to provide for them and can't assist with homework; for others, this means they help too much with homework because they think that is best. We have never met a caregiver who is not trying the best he or she knows how. Sometimes it falls on us to help him or her see other ways to do so.

2. **Own the mindset that we don't just have a certain child in our class, we have a whole family along with that child.** When we provide families with strategies that support organization, social skills, and instruction, we have a better chance of impacting a child in the long term. Blogs and newsletters that provide classroom charts, step-by-step strategies, and how-to videos filmed by kids can help do this. (See *Amplify* by Katie Muhtaris and Kristin Ziemke [2015] for more on technology in the classroom.)

3. **Though we may be the experts on instruction, families are the experts on their children.** Don't just ask questions, use the answers. If you learn a child tends to nap on the weekends, that may tell you they need a rest after lunch in the classroom. If you learn a child only sees a specific caregiver on Tuesdays, you may learn that Tuesdays can be challenging days for her.

4. **Do you teach a child with challenging behaviors? Be honest and objective with the family.** It is not about the child as a person, it is about the behaviors he employs. A child is never bad, but his behaviors may be counterproductive to learning and getting along with others. Keep conversations centered on actionable, changeable aspects of behavior, and not about the child as a human being.

5. **Make your room a community space!** If your school allows it, have families come in for projects or celebrations or just to watch the classroom in action. If possible, vary the times and days of the week, or have a sign-up so that working families can find a time and day that works for them. Give as much advance notice as possible so that families can try to take time off work.

6. **Offer various forms of communication.** Not all families will have access to computers, and smart phones may have limited data plans. We are a huge fan of blogs, twitter, and email, but you may also want to provide printouts of any electronic communication for those who need them.

7. **Build relationships.** This seems obvious, but it is not always easy when your plate is so full. Celebrate as a community when a baby is born, a tooth is lost, or someone gets a new job. Likewise, offer your sympathies when a loss happens, or difficulties occur. This is not to say you should pry, but rather see families as people first and partners in your job. Be warm, be welcoming, be humane.

 Scan this QR code or visit hein.pub/kidsfirst-login to access reproducible versions of the appendixes. (Enter your email address and password or click "Create a New Account" to set up an account. Once you have logged in, enter keycode KIDSFIRST2018 and click "Register.")

Annotated First-Day Letter

Dear Families,

Welcome to kindergarten! This is a very exciting time and I so look forward to getting to know you and your child(ren). Together we can ensure a successful school year. This packet contains important information for accomplishing that.

About Me

My name is _____. I am delighted to be your child's teacher this year! There are a variety of ways to reach me: (email) (school phone). Please feel free to reach me with questions, concerns, and stories and I will get back to you as soon as I can. I believe that play is at the heart of all learning and that each child has a unique learning path. Some articles that reflect my beliefs can be found at _____ .

About Kindergarten

We want all children to leave kindergarten with the requisite skills in literacy and math, as well as with an active learning stance, which means that *students* develop questions and pursue answers *independently*. Learning is an active (and sometimes messy) process. Play and inquiry are important components of developing this burgeoning literacy and mathematical sense, as well as the main ways children sustain and refine the larger stances of critical thinking, problem solving, independence, and questioning. Kindergarten is one of the most magical years of schooling. Children enter at a variety of developmental stages and emerge reading, writing, and applying number sense to the world around them.

Additionally this is a time of important social growth. Your child will be part of a community that values empathy, joy, and respect. Just like reading and writing, these skills are taught in our classroom, and I look forward to sharing with you the growth we make as citizens of the world.

Aim for words like *families* or phrases like *fifth-grade community* to be inclusive of all family dynamics. Every child won't live with parents.

This packet might include a family survey or questionnaire, along with anything your school might require. This could all be done online via Google Docs or other apps.

Make sure families know you want them involved for the "good stuff" and not just issues.

Providing links or resources that ground your belief system in research can be helpful for parents. The *Atlantic, EdWeek, Mind/Shift, Community Playthings*, youcubed.org, and other blogs often have parent-friendly articles. If you have families who do not use English as a home language, you could send home information in their preferred language.

Use this opportunity to establish your beliefs that behavior is also learned and that teaching about being a citizen will be an active part of your classroom.

Or whatever grade you teach. Remember—families may only have a vague sense of expectations (or fears!) at each grade. It can be helpful to give families a big picture, with lots of reassurance that you will help make it happen.

May be photocopied for classroom use. © 2019 by Christine Hertz and Kristine Mraz from *Kids First from Day One*. Portsmouth, NH: Heinemann.

A first-day letter can send many messages about you, about your classroom, and your view of parents. Giving some general recommendations to families can help them see that you value them as partners in this journey.

About Supporting Kindergarten Work at Home

We are a homework-free school! However, many families have asked about things they can do anytime to support their child's growing brain.

★ **Read books together.** Any chance you get, read a book to or with your child. Besides a great opportunity to bond, this helps your child develop a love of reading and healthy reading habits.

★ **Tell sequenced stories, retell events.** Stories can help children understand who they are in the world and help them make sense of events around them. Model this for your child by telling stories to him or her: the trip to the store, the day he or she was born, the time he or she saw a giant bug. Encourage the child to tell the story with you. Children's oral language and vocabulary development explode between the ages of three and six; take advantage of this and talk, talk, talk.

★ **Make writing tools available and encourage children to write lists, cards, stories, labels—anything really!** Children will go through several stages of spelling before they become "conventional spellers." Scribbling leads to letterlike shapes, then to actual letters, and then to more conventional writing. Each step has a place, and the most important thing you can do as a parent is to encourage children to write no matter what it looks like. The more children attempt (even if it is just scribbles), the more they practice and gain confidence. Over time, children will develop a myriad of ways to write and spell, but only if they are first accustomed to taking risks and making a few mistakes!

★ **Count everything, everywhere.** When unpacking groceries, count each item; when lining up stuffed animals, count them. Guess how many dogs you will see walking to school and then count to find out. Try using words like *more*, *less*, *same*. These basic activities are laying the groundwork for number sense.

★ **Have fun and play often!**

About Your Child

You are your child's first and most important teacher, and so I would like to learn from you more about him or her and how best he or she learns. I would appreciate it if you could take a few minutes to fill out the questionnaire below.

I look forward to our journey together this year. Please feel free to contact me at any time. Your children are precious, and I take your entrusting them to my care seriously and with my whole heart.

Controversial! There is a lot of interesting research about this, but if you are looking for some great ideas about homework, check out *No More Mindless Homework* by Kathy Collins and Joanne Bempechat (2017).

When you make your questionnaire, consider what information you will really value and use. Play style? Preferences? Ease in large groups? Feelings about change? Think beyond academics and try to get at some of the insider information only a family member can provide.

Annotated Letter About Mindset

Dear Families,

It is with great pleasure that we welcome you and your child into our community for the _____ school year. As we learn and play together, we will also be building critical skills for a lifetime of curiosity and growth. We will be teaching some important ways of thinking about ourselves and the world this year that have grown out of the incredible work of Carol Dweck.

Carol Dweck is a researcher, currently at Stanford University, who has pioneered a great deal of work around the idea of growth mindset. A growth mindset is the belief that we can learn anything with support, hard work, and thoughtful strategic instruction. Children with a growth mindset outperform children who do not think of themselves and their learning in this way.

The way we support this work in our classroom is by intentionally teaching ways of thinking about ourselves and our ways of learning. This year, we will be teaching your children the concepts of:

★ **Optimism:** The belief that no matter the obstacle, we have the power and possibility to overcome it.

★ **Resilience:** The ability to bounce back from setbacks and frustrations and learn from them when they happen.

★ **Persistence:** The habit of trying something more than once, or sticking with something through the hard parts.

★ **Flexibility:** The knowledge that there are multiple ways to solve any problem, and the skills to strategically solve it.

★ **Empathy:** The ability to understand feelings and other people's points of view. A fundamental aspect of a healthy child and a healthy community.

As we learn more about these big ideas, we will think about ways to use self-talk, self stories, goal setting, and reflection to reinforce and support these positive habits of mind. Stay tuned for that work as it unfolds.

As in all things, you are our greatest partners, and so we invite you on this journey with us! We'll be introducing these concepts slowly over the course of the next few weeks and let you know when we do so. Here are some ways you can support and connect with your child over these big ideas:

★ **Share your own stories.** Talk with your child about times you showed empathy or were flexible.

Some schools and classrooms have invited families to join a book study of Carol Dweck's work.

Carol Dweck states this information in "Carol Dweck Revisits the 'Growth Mindset'" (2015).

This list can also include important ideas like self-management, compassion, organization, or cooperation. It is up to you and what your children need.

Also stay tuned for some more sample letters about things like self-talk and storytelling.

As you introduce each stance, you could send a note home to families saying something such as, "This week we started a conversation about ____ by reading ____. Together, as a class, we defined ____ as ____. We'll continue to explore this stance this week by ____. At home you could ____."

We've included the phrase *strategic instruction* to reinforce the idea that feedback and instruction from teachers are important components of developing our students' mindsets. For more on Dweck's latest work, check out Dweck (2016b).

★ **Listen in on your own self-talk and refine it.** Be mindful of saying things like "I can't" as in "I can't put together this IKEA furniture!" Instead try, "This feels hard, but I am going to take a break and try it a different way to see if that helps!"

★ **Read with your child** and talk about the ways characters are acting with regard to these habits of mind.

★ **Read more about this!** At the end of this letter you will find a list of links to articles and titles. Most are short and (hopefully) interesting, and they can give you some of the background about the work we're doing.

We look forward to talking with you more as the year unfolds. As always, feel free to contact us with questions, comments, and concerns. It is with great pleasure that we begin this journey together.

Warmly,

> You might also consider sending these articles out to families in newsletters and emails over the course of a few weeks.

For more information:

- "Carol Dweck Revisits the 'Growth Mindset'" (Dweck 2015): www.edweek.org/ew/articles/2015/09/23/carol-dweck-revisits-the -growth-mindset.html)

- "Researchers Studied Kindergarteners' Behavior and Followed Up 19 Years Later. Here Are the Findings." (Porter 2015): www.upworthy .com/researchers-studied-kindergarteners-behavior-and-followed-up -19-years-later-here-are-the-findings

- "Reading Harry Potter Books Can Make Kids More Tolerant" (Yahoo Health 2014): www.yahoo.com/beauty/reading-harry-potter-books -can-make-kids-more-tolerant-93438785457.html

- "Why Parents Need to Let Their Children Fail: A New Study Explores What Happens to Students Who Aren't Allowed to Suffer through Setbacks" (Lahey 2013): www.theatlantic.com/national /archive/2013/01/why-parents-need-to-let-their-children-fail/272603

- "How Not to Talk to Your Kids: The Inverse Power of Praise" (Bronson 2007): http://nymag.com/news/features/27840

Room Planning Guide

Ask yourself:

★ Do I have small and intimate spaces where children can work alone and focus?

★ Do I have large spaces where children can work collaboratively?

★ Do I have an ease of movement between spaces?

★ Are materials that I want children to access easy to get to and attractively displayed?

★ Are my materials hidden away or in a space that is not convenient for children?

★ Do I have flexible and moveable seating?

★ Does my "stuff" take up very little space?

★ Do I have open spaces for movement or building?

★ When I look at my room from a child's height, what do I see?

Sketch space:

Quick Guide to Teaching Social Skills

Skill: _____

★ What do we (my students and I) understand about this skill?
  What is a reasonable expectation for children of this age when it comes to this skill?

★ What are the steps involved? What does this skill look like when it is done proficiently?
  What is hard about this skill?

★ What are the reasons this skill is beneficial to the people using it?

★ How will I teach it and reinforce it?

WHOLE-CLASS CONVERSATION AND REFLECTION	READ-ALOUDS AND STORYTELLING	VISUALIZATION AND ROLE-PLAYING

Quick Guide to Dealing with Challenging Behaviors

∙∙∙∙∙∙∙∙∙∙ ∙ ∙∙∙∙∙∙∙∙∙∙∙∙∙∙∙∙∙∙∙ ∙ ∙∙∙∙∙

Questions to ask when studying a child's behavior:

★ How often do the challenging behaviors occur?

★ Are there specific times during the day or days of the week when you see the behaviors?

★ If you notice that the behaviors happen more on Tuesday mornings or Thursday afternoons, can you determine if there's anything different about those days at school or at home?

★ Are the behaviors more present when certain children or adults are present?

★ Are there any fine/gross motor actions that seem to trigger the behaviors?

★ In which places in the school (and classroom) do the behaviors occur?

★ Do these behaviors occur more often during structured or unstructured times?

★ Are there any biological factors at play? Food? Sleep patterns?

★ What are you expecting the child to be doing when the behaviors occur?

STEPS FOR SOLVING UNSOLVED PROBLEMS

STEP	PROCESS	KEY PHRASES
1. Empathize	For the first step, Greene suggests that we start the conversation by saying, "I've noticed that . . . What's up?" He writes, "The goal of the empathy step is to achieve the best possible understanding of a kid's concern or perspective related to a given problem" (Greene 2008, 79). Of course, there will be many times where a child will not be able to tell you—or is not at all aware of—the why behind her behavioral challenges. In those cases, there's no reason to skip over the empathy step. There's no harm in asking and there's no harm in saying, "It can feel really hard . . ."	I've noticed that . . . What's up? Can you say more about that? What do you mean?
2. Define adult concern	This is the step in the process where you identify the unsolved problem. Greene urges teachers to make sure this isn't a time to dwell on rules or even to focus on the solution to the problem. Instead, it should focus on how the problem is affecting the student or other people (Greene 2008, 90). It may feel hard to pull back or not sound judgmental in this step. This is a good time to remind yourself that at this moment your upstairs brain might be harder to access as well.	I think I know what you're saying. The thing is . . . I hear you. The tricky thing is . . .
3. Invitation	The final step is where you work collaboratively to solve the problem. "The Invitation lets the kid know that solving the problem is something you're doing *with* him—in other words together—rather than to him" (Greene 2008, 92–93). At the end of this step, you'll have a realistic goal that works for both of you.	I wonder if there's a way for us to solve this problem. I wonder how you could . . . Is that something you'd like to do? Do you want to give that a try?

STEPS FOR HANDLING ESPECIALLY CHALLENGING MOMENTS

STEP	WHAT IT IS	KEY PHRASES
1. Get to yes	When a child is operating solely in his downstairs (think fight-or-flight) brain, our first step is to get him to start using his upstairs, or logical brain. These questions are like "contact statements" to help you reconnect these areas of the brain. Ask a series of questions that get him to say (or yell), "Yes" (Goulston 2009, 206).	Are you really mad right now? Are you angry at me? Do you really hate reading right now?
2. Name it	Next, name the problem in simple, nonjudgmental terms. This should be another opportunity to get him to say, "Yes."	You're really mad because . . .
3. Scale it	Help the child identify where in her body she's feeling the strong emotion or ask her to scale it from small to big with her hands. Even if the problem seems very small to you, the reflective work of thinking through the problem is what's reactivating her upstairs brain.	How upset are you? Show me with your hands how upset you are. Where in your body are you feeling really upset? Point to it.
4. Solve it	Your main goal now is to develop a plan that enables the child to regulate, stay safe, and rejoin the group. This might mean taking a break away in a quiet corner of a classroom or going for a walk. Rocking, rhythms, bouncing a ball, or doing something repetitive in nature can help a child regulate, too. When a child has regulated (which might take quite some time or might not even be until the next day), you can help guide him through a reflective process to think about how he might have solved the problem in a different way. This is another great opportunity for role-playing and practice.	The reason you're so mad is because . . . I know you're mad, but can you solve this problem with me? Here's a space for you to get calm. Come see me when you feel ready to make a plan.

Checklist Template

....

_____ **Checklist**

Conference Notes Form

· ·

_____ **Conferring Notes**   **Week** _____

Conferring and Small-Group Planning Grid

Next Step: _____

Children:

Notes:

Next Step: _____

Children:

Notes:

Next Step: _____

Children:

Notes:

Next Step: _____

Children:

Notes:

Next Step: _____

Children:

Notes:

Next Step: _____

Children:

Notes:

Next Step: _____

Children:

Notes:

Next Step: _____

Children:

Notes:

Works Cited

Adichie, Chimamanda. 2009. "The Danger of a Single Story." TED Talk, July. www.ted.com /talks/chimamanda_adichie_the_danger_of_a_single_story.

Ahmed. Sara. 2018 *Being the Change: Lessons and Strategies to Teach Social Comprehension*. Portsmouth, NH: Heinemann.

American Psychological Association. "Is Willpower a Limited Resource?" www.apa.org /helpcenter/willpower-limited-resource.pdf.

Anderson, Carl. 2000. *How's It Going? A Practical Guide to Conferring with Student Writers*. Portsmouth, NH: Heinemann.

———. 2015. *Assessing Writers*. Portsmouth, NH: Heinemann.

Angelillo, Janet. 2008. *Whole-Class Teaching: Minilessons and More*. Portsmouth, NH: Heinemann.

Association of Psychological Science. 2014. "Heavily Decorated Classrooms Disrupt Attention and Learning in Young Children." *APS Online*. www.psychologicalscience.org /news/releases/heavily-decorated-classrooms-disrupt-attention-and-learning-in-young -children.html#.WCYLJWPl5lI.

Baker, Jean A., Sycarah Grant, and Larissa Morlock. 2008. "The Teacher-Student Relationship as a Developmental Context for Children with Internalizing or Externalizing Behavior Problems." *School Psychology Quarterly* 23: 3–15.

Baker, Jed. 2001. *The Social Skills Picture Book: Teaching Play, Emotion, and Communication to Children with Autism*. Arlington, TX: Future Horizons.

Baumeister, Roy F., Kathleen Vohs, and Dianne M. Tice. 2007. "The Strength Model of Self-Control." *Current Directions in Psychological Science* 16 (6): 351–55.

Beers, Kylene, and Robert Probst. 2012. *Notice & Note: Strategies for Close Reading*. Portsmouth, NH: Heinemann.

Brown, Brené. 2012. "Listening to Shame." TED Talk, March. www.ted.com/talks /brene_brown_listening_to_shame.

Brown, Stuart, and Christopher Vaughan. 2010. *Play: How It Shapes the Brain, Opens the Imagination, and Invigorates the Soul*. New York: Penguin Group.

Brown, Sunni. 2014. *The Doodle Revolution: Unlock the Power to Think Differently*. New York: Portfolio Penguin.

Bunn, Tom. 2016. "When Anxious, Our Most Basic Strategy Is to Run." www.psychologytoday.com/blog/conquer-fear-flying/201610 /when-anxious-our-most-basic-strategy-is-run.

Calkins, Lucy. 1994. *The Art of Teaching Writing*. Portsmouth, NH: Heinemann.

———. 2000. *The Art of Teaching Reading*. New York: Pearson.

———. 2014. *Writing Pathways: Performance Assessments and Learning Progressions, Grades K–8*. Portsmouth, NH: Heinemann.

Calkins, Lucy and colleagues. 2015. Units of Study for Teaching Reading Series, Grades K–5: A Grade-by-Grade Workshop Curriculum. Portsmouth, NH; Heinemann.

———. 2016. Units of Study in Opinion, Information, and Narrative Writing Elementary Series, Grades K–5: A Workshop Curriculum. Portsmouth, NH: Heinemann.

Calkins, Lucy, Amanda Hartman, and Zoë Ryder White. 2005. *One to One: The Art of Conferring with Young Writers*. Portsmouth, NH: Heinemann.

Caple, Kathy. 2000. *Worm Is Stuck*. Cambridge, MA: Candlewick Press.

Carlson, Frances M. 2011. *Big Body Play: Why Boisterous, Vigorous, and Very Physical Play Is Essential to Children's Development and Learning*. Washington, DC: NAEYC.

Cassetta, Gianna, and Brook Sawyer. 2015. *Classroom Management Matters: The Social–Emotional Learning Approach Children Deserve*. Portsmouth, NH: Heinemann.

Ceppi, Giulio, and Michele Zini, eds. 1998. *Children, Spaces, Relations: Metaproject for an Environment for Young Children*. Reggio Emilia, Italy: Reggio Children.

Clay, Marie M. 2016. *Literacy Lessons Designed for Individuals*. 2d ed. Portsmouth, NH: Heinemann.

———. 2017. *Running Records for Classroom Teachers*. 2d ed. Portsmouth, NH: Heinemann.

Cole, Susan F., Jessica Greenwald O'Brien, M. Geron Gadd, Joel Ristuccia, D. Luray Wallace, and Michael Gregory. 2005. *Helping Traumatized Children Learn: Supportive School Environments for Children Traumatized by Family Violence*. https://traumasensitiveschools .org/wp-content/uploads/2013/06/Helping-Traumatized-Children-Learn.pdf.

Collins, Kathy. 2004. *Growing Readers: Units of Study in the Primary Classroom*. Portland, ME: Stenhouse.

Collins, Kathy, and Matt Glover. 2015. *I Am Reading: Nurturing Young Children's Meaning Making and Joyful Engagement with Any Book*. Portsmouth, NH: Heinemann.

Connell, Gill, and Cheryl McCarthy. 2013. *A Moving Child is a Learning Child: How the Body Teaches the Brain to Think*. Golden Valley, MN: Free Spirit Publishing.

Cruz, Colleen. 2004. *Independent Writing: One Teacher—Thirty-Two Needs, Topics, and Plans*. Portsmouth, NH: Heinemann.

Curtis, Deb, and Margie Carter. 2011. *Reflecting Children's Lives: A Handbook for Planning Your Child-Centered Curriculum*. 2d ed. St. Paul, MN: Redleaf Press.

———. 2014. *Designs for Living and Learning: Transforming Early Childhood Environments*. 2d ed. St. Paul, MN: Redleaf Press.

Daniels, Harvey "Smokey". 2017. *The Curious Classroom: 10 Structures for Teaching with Student-Directed Inquiry*. Portsmouth, NH: Heinemann.

Daniels, Harvey "Smokey", and Sara Ahmed. 2014. *Upstanders: How to Engage Middle School Hearts and Minds with Inquiry*. Portsmouth, NH: Heinemann.

Dean, Jeremy. 2013. *Making Habits, Breaking Habits: Why We Do Things, Why We Don't, and How to Make Any Change Stick*. Boston, MA: Da Capo Press.

Derman-Sparks, Louise, and Julie Olsen Edwards. 2009. *Anti-Bias Education for Young Children and Ourselves*. Washington, DC: National Association for the Education of Young Children.

Dewey, John. 1922. "Morals Are Human." In *Human Nature and Conduct: An Introduction to Social Psychology*. New York: Modern Library.

Dierking, Connie, and Sherra Jones. 2014. *Oral Mentor Texts: A Powerful Tool for Teaching Reading, Writing, Speaking, and Listening*. Portsmouth, NH: Heinemann.

Dillard, Annie. 1989. *The Writing Life*. New York: Harper & Row.

Dinnerstein, Renée. 2016. *Choice Time: How to Deepen Learning Through Inquiry and Play, PreK–2*. Portsmouth, NH: Heinemann.

Dods, Jennifer. 2013. "Enhancing Understanding of the Nature of Supportive School-based Relationships for Youth Who Have Experienced Trauma." *Canadian Journal of Education* 36: 71–95.

Dweck, Carol. 2008. *Mindset: The New Psychology of Success*. New York: Ballantine.

———. 2015. "Carol Dweck Revisits the 'Growth Mindset.'" *Education Week*. www.edweek.org/ew/articles/2015/09/23/carol-dweck-revisits-the-growth-mindset.html.

———. 2016a. "The Journey to a Growth Mindset: Carol Dweck's Live Keynote Presentation." https://youtube/kuq91hqUvBg.

———. 2016b. Learning and the Brain Conference, February. San Francisco.

Fecser, Mary Ellen. 2015. "Classroom Strategies for Traumatized, Oppositional Students." *Reclaiming Children & Youth* 24 (1): 20–24.

Fletcher, Ralph, and JoAnn Portalupi. 2001. *Writing Workshop: The Essential Guide*. Portsmouth, NH: Heinemann.

Flora, Carlin. 2006. "Self-Portrait in a Skewed Mirror." *Psychology Today Online*. www.psychologytoday.com/articles/200601/self-portrait-in-skewed-mirror.

Fondas, Nonette. 2014. "You Really Can Work Smarter, Not Harder." *The Atlantic Online*. www.theatlantic.com/education/archive/2014/05/study-you-really-can-work-smarter-not-harder/370819.

Fosnot, Catherine Twomey and Maarten Dolk. 2001a. *Young Mathematicians at Work: Constructing Number Sense, Addition, and Subtraction*. Portsmouth, NH: Heinemann.

———. 2001b. *Young Mathematicians at Work: Constructing Multiplication and Division*. Portsmouth, NH: Heinemann.

———. 2002. *Young Mathematicians at Work: Constructing Fractions, Decimals, and Percents*. Portsmouth, NH: Heinemann.

Fountas, Irene C., and Gay Su Pinnell. 2016. *Guided Reading: Responsive Teaching Across the Grades*. 2d ed. Portsmouth, NH: Heinemann.

———. 2017. *Prompting Guide*. Portsmouth, NH: Heinemann.

Gallas, Karen. 1995. *Talking Their Way into Science: Hearing Children's Questions and Theories, Responding with Curricula*. New York: Teachers College Press.

Gandini, Lella. 1998. "Education and Caring Spaces." In *The Hundred Languages of Children*. Edited by Carolyn Edwards, Lella Gandini, and George Forman. Greenwich, CT: Ablex.

Gilliam, Walter S., Angela N. Maupin, Chin R. Reyes, Maria Accaritti, and Frederick Shic. 2016. "Do Early Educators' Implicit Biases Regarding Sex and Race Relate to Behavior Expectations and Recommendations of Preschool Expulsions and Suspensions?" New Haven, CT: Yale University Child Study Center.

Glover, Matt, and Mary Alice Berry. 2012. *Projecting Possibilities for Writers: The How, What, and Why of Designing Units of Study, K–5*. Portsmouth, NH: Heinemann.

Goulston, Mark. 2009. *Just Listen: Discover the Secret to Getting Through to Absolutely Anyone*. New York: AMACOM.

Gray, Carol. 2015. *The New Social Story Book: Over 150 Social Stories that Teach Everyday Social Skills to Children and Adults with Autism and their Peers*. Revised and Expanded 15th Anniversary Edition. Arlington, TX: Future Horizons, Inc.

Greene, Ross. 2008. *Lost at School: Why Our Kids with Behavioral Challenges Are Falling Through the Cracks and How We Can Help Them*. New York: Scribner.

Hare, Rebecca Louise, and Robert Dillon. 2016. *The Space: A Guide for Educators*. Irvine, CA: EdTech Team Press.

Harvey, Stephanie, and Harvey "Smokey" Daniels. 2015. *Comprehension and Collaboration: Inquiry Circles for Curiosity, Engagement, and Understanding*. Portsmouth, NH: Heinemann.

Harvey, Stephanie, and Anne Goudvis. 2017. *Strategies That Work: Teaching Comprehension for Understanding, Engagement, and Building Knowledge*. Portland, ME: Stenhouse.

Hattie, John, and Gregory C. R. Yates. 2013. *Visible Learning and the Science of How We Learn*. New York: Routledge.

Heard, Georgia, and Jennifer McDonough. 2009. *A Place for Wonder: Reading and Writing Nonfiction in the Primary Grades*. Portland, ME: Stenhouse.

Henkes, Kevin. 2008. *Chrysanthemum*. New York: Mulberry Books.

Hubbard, Ruth Shagoury, and Brenda Miller Power. 2003. *The Art of Classroom Inquiry: A Handbook for Teacher–Researchers*. Portsmouth, NH: Heinemann.

Kittle, Penny. 2012. *Book Love: Developing Depth, Stamina, and Passion in Adolescent Readers*. Portsmouth, NH: Heinemann.

Landrigan, Clare, and Tammy Mulligan. 2018. *It's All About the Books: How to Create Bookrooms and Classroom Libraries that Inspire Readers*. Portsmouth, NH: Heinemann.

Lewis, Katherine Reynolds. 2015. "What If Everything You Knew About Discipline Was Wrong?" *Mother Jones*. www.motherjones.com/politics/2015/07 /schools-behavior-discipline-collaborative-proactive-solutions-ross-greene.

Lifshitz, Jessica (@Jess5th). 2016. "The faces that greet our students from our bookshelves can be as powerful as the ones that greet them at the door." Twitter, August 15, 3:39 p.m. https://twitter.com/Jess5th/status/765316926885154816.

Lipsky, Laura van Dernoot, and Connie Burk. 2009. *Trauma Stewardship: An Everyday Guide to Caring for Self While Caring for Others*. Oakland, CA: Berrett-Koehler Publishers.

Malaguzzi, Loris. 1998. "History, Ideas, and Basic Philosophy." In *The Hundred Languages of Children*. Edited by Carolyn Edwards, Lella Gandini, and George Forman. Greenwich, CT: Ablex.

Marchetti, Allison, and Rebekah O'Dell. 2015. *Writing with Mentors: How to Reach Every Writer in the Room Using Current, Engaging Mentor Texts*. Portsmouth, NH; Heinemann.

Martinelli, Marjorie, and Kristine Mraz. 2012. *Smarter Charts, K–2: Optimizing an Instructional Staple to Create Independent Readers and Writers*. Portsmouth, NH: Heinemann.

McGinnis, Ellen. 2011. *Skillstreaming the Elementary School Child: A Guide for Teaching Prosocial Skills*. Champaign, IL: Research Press.

Meier, Deborah. 2013. "Alfie Kohn: Why Punishment Doesn't Work." http://blogs.edweek .org/edweek/Bridging-Differences/2013/01/guest_blogger_alfie_kohn_joins.html.

Mermelstein, Leah. 2007. *Don't Forget to Share: The Crucial Last Step in the Writing Workshop*. Portsmouth, NH: Heinemann.

Moses, Lindsey, and Meridith Ogden. 2017. *What Are the Rest of My Kids Doing? Fostering Independence in the K–2 Reading Workshop*. Portsmouth, NH: Heinemann.

Mraz, Kristine, and Christine Hertz. 2015. *A Mindset for Learning: Teaching the Traits of Joyful, Independent Growth*. Portsmouth, NH: Heinemann.

Mraz, Kristine, and Marjorie Martinelli. 2014. *Smarter Charts for Math, Science, and Social Studies: Making Learning Visible in the Content Areas*. Portsmouth, NH: Heinemann.

Mraz, Kristine, Alison Porcelli, and Cheryl Tyler. 2016. *Purposeful Play: A Teacher's Guide to Igniting Deep and Joyful Learning Across the Day*. Portsmouth, NH: Heinemann.

Muhtaris, Katie, and Kristin Ziemke. 2015. *Amplify: Digital Teaching and Learning in the K–6 Classroom*. Portsmouth, NH: Heinemann.

National Child Traumatic Stress Network Schools Committee. 2008. *Child Trauma Toolkit for Educators*. Los Angeles, CA and Durham, NC: National Center for Child Traumatic Stress.

Neff, Kristin. 2011. *Self-Compassion: Stop Beating Yourself Up and Leave Insecurity Behind*. New York: William Morrow.

Nin, Anaïs. 1961. *The Seduction of the Minotaur*. Victoria, British Columbia: The Swallow Press.

NPREd. 2016. "Bias Isn't Just a Police Problem, It's a Preschool Problem." www.npr.org/sections/ed/2016/09/28/495488716/bias-isnt-just-a-police-prolem-its-a -preschool-problem

O'Connell, Susan, Marcy Myers, and John SanGiovanni. 2016. *Math in Practice: Teaching Kindergarten Math*. Portsmouth, NH: Heinemann.

O'Connell, Susan, Laura Hunovice, and John SanGiovanni. 2016. *Math in Practice: Teaching First-Grade Math*. Portsmouth, NH: Heinemann.

O'Connell, Susan, Allison Peet, and John SanGiovanni. 2016. *Math in Practice: Teaching Second-Grade Math*. Portsmouth, NH: Heinemann.

O'Connell, Susan, Cheryl Akers, and John SanGiovanni. 2016. *Math in Practice: Teaching Third-Grade Math*. Portsmouth, NH: Heinemann.

O'Connell, Susan, Kay B. Sammons, and John SanGiovanni. 2016. *Math in Practice: Teaching Fourth-Grade Math*. Portsmouth, NH: Heinemann.

O'Connell, Susan, Joan Petti Tellish, and John SanGiovanni. 2016. *Math in Practice: Teaching Fifth-Grade Math*. Portsmouth, NH: Heinemann.

Olds, Anita. 2000. *Child Care Design Guide*. New York: McGraw-Hill.

Perry, Phillippa. 2012. *How to Stay Sane*. New York: Picador Press.

Pink, Daniel H. 2011. *Drive: The Surprising Truth About What Motivates Us*. New York: Riverhead Books.

Plumb, Jacqui L., Kelly A. Bush, and Sonia E. Kersevich. 2016. "Trauma-Sensitive Schools: An Evidence-Based Approach." *School Social Work Journal* 40 (2): 37–60.

Porcelli, Alison, and Cheryl Tyler. 2008. *A Quick Guide to Boosting English Acquisition in Choice Time, K–2*. Portsmouth, NH: Heinemann.

Pranikoff, Kara. 2017. *Teaching Talk: A Practical Guide to Fostering Student Thinking and Conversation*. Portsmouth, NH: Heinemann.

Rahim, Masuma. 2014. "Developmental Trauma Disorder: An Attachment-Based Perspective." *Clinical Child Psychology and Psychiatry* 19 (4): 548–60.

Randell, Beverley, Jenny Giles, and Annette Smith. 1996. *The Go-Carts*. Boston, MA: Rigby PM collection/Houghton Mifflin Harcourt.

Ray, Katie Wood, and Lisa B. Cleaveland. 2004. *About the Authors: Writing Workshop with Our Youngest Writers*. Portsmouth, NH: Heinemann.

Ray, Katie Wood, and Matt Glover. 2008. *Already Ready: Nurturing Writers in Preschool and Kindergarten*. Portsmouth, NH; Heinemann.

Responsive Classroom. 2015. *The First Six Weeks of School*. 2d ed. Turners Falls, MA: Center for Responsive Schools, Inc.

Roberts, Kate, and Maggie Beattie Roberts. 2016. *DIY Literacy: Teaching Tools for Differentiation, Rigor, and Independence*. Portsmouth, NH: Heinemann.

Rosenfeld, Malke. 2016. *Math on the Move: Engaging Students in Whole Body Learning*. Portsmouth, NH: Heinemann.

Rossen, Eric, and Robert Hull, eds. 2012. *Supporting and Educating Traumatized Students: A Guide for School-Based Professionals*. New York: Oxford University Press.

Roy, Arundhati. 2008. *The God of Small Things*. New York: Random House.

Safford, Victoria. 2014. "The Small Work in the Great Work." In *The Impossible Will Take a Little While: Perseverance and Hope in Troubled Times*. Edited by Paul Rogat Loeb. New York: Basic Books.

Schwartz, Katrina. 2015. "Why Kids Need to Move, Touch and Experience to Learn." ww2 .kqed.org/mindshift/2015/03/26/why-kids-need-to-move-touch-and-experience-to-learn.

Scott, Lakia M., and Barbara Purdum-Cassidy, eds. 2016. *Culturally Affirming Literacy Practices for Urban Elementary Students*. Lanham, MD: Rowman & Littlefield.

Serafini, Frank. 2001. *The Reading Workshop: Creating Space for Readers*. Portsmouth, NH: Heinemann.

Serravallo, Jennifer. 2010. *Teaching Reading in Small Groups: Differentiated Instruction for Building Strategic, Independent Readers*. Portsmouth, NH: Heinemann.

———. 2015. *The Reading Strategies Book: Your Everything Guide to Developing Skilled Readers*. Portsmouth, NH: Heinemann.

———. 2017. *The Writing Strategies Book: Your Everything Guide to Developing Skilled Writers*. Portsmouth, NH: Heinemann.

Serravallo, Jennifer, and Gravity Goldberg. 2007. *Conferring with Readers: Supporting Each Student's Growth and Independence*. Portsmouth, NH: Heinemann.

Shonkoff, Jack P., and Andrew S. Garner. 2012. "The Lifelong Effects of Early Childhood Adversity and Toxic Stress." *Pediatrics* 129: 232–46.

Siegel, Daniel, and Tina Payne Bryson. 2012. *The Whole Brain Child: 12 Revolutionary Strategies to Nurture Your Child's Developing Mind*. New York: Delacorte Press.

Spiegel, Alex. 2012. "Teachers' Expectations Can Influence How Students Perform." www.npr.org/sections/health-shots/2012/09/18/161159263 /teachers-expectations-can-influence-how-students-perform.

Stulberg, Brad. 2016. "Big Goals Can Backfire. Olympians Show Us What to Focus on Instead." http://nymag.com/scienceofus/2016/08/why-having-big-goals-can-backfire .html.

Turner, Cory. NPR. "Bias Isn't Just a Police Problem, It's a Preschool Problem." www.npr.org/sections/ed/2016/09/28/495488716 /bias-isnt-just-a-police-problem-its-a-preschool-problem.

Van der Kolk, Bessel. 2015. *The Body Keeps the Score: Brain, Mind, and Body in the Healing of Trauma*. New York: Penguin Books.

Vygotsky, Lev S. 1978. *Mind In Society: The Development of Higher Psychological Processes*. Cambridge, MA: Harvard University Press.

Wardle, Francis. 2016. "The Challenge of Boys in Early Childhood Education." *Community Playthings*. www.communityplaythings.com/resources/articles/2016 /boys-in-early-childhood-education.

Wiseman, Theresa. 1996. "A Concept Analysis of Empathy." *Journal of Advanced Nursing* 23 (6): 1162–67.

Wood, Chip. 2007. *Yardsticks: Children in the Classroom Ages 4-14*. 3rd ed. Turners Falls, MA: Center for Responsive Schools, Inc.

Wurm, Julianne. 2005. *Working in the Reggio Way: A Beginner's Guide for American Teachers*. St. Paul, MN: Redleaf Press.

Zane, Linda M. 2015. *Pedagogy and Space: Design Inspirations for Early Childhood Classrooms*. St. Paul, MN: Redleaf Press.

Zemelman, Steven. 2016. *From Inquiry to Action: Civic Engagement with Project-Based Learning in All Content Areas*. Portsmouth, NH: Heinemann.